Corpsmen

Corps

men
Letters from Korea

Richard G. Chappell

& Gerald E. Chappell

The Kent State

University Press

KENT, OHIO, & LONDON

© 2000 by

The Kent State University Press, Kent, Ohio 44242

ALL RIGHTS RESERVED

Library of Congress Catalog Card Number 00-29580

ISBN 0-87338-669-8

Manufactured in the United States of America

07 06 05 04 03 02 01 00   5 4 3 2 1

Library of Congress Cataloging-in-Publication Data

Chappell, Richard G., 1932–1998.

Corpsmen : letters from Korea / Richard G. Chappell and Gerald E. Chappell.

p.   cm.

Includes bibliographical references.

ISBN 0-87338-669-8 (cloth : alk. paper) ∞

1. Korean War, 1950–1953—Personal narratives, American.   2. Korean War, 1950–1953—Medical care—United States.   3. Chappell, Richard G., 1932–1998—Correspondence.   4. Chappell, Gerald E. (Gerald Eugene), 1932– —Correspondence.   5. United States. Navy—Hospital corpsmen—Biography. 6. Indochinese War, 1946–1954—Personal narratives.   I. Chappell, Gerald E. (Gerald Eugene), 1932– .   II. Title.

DS921.6 .C386   2000

951.904'2'092—dc21

00-029580

British Library Cataloging-in-Publication data are available.

Contents

Acknowledgments

We thank Anne Dyken, Christine Chappell, Steven Chappell, and John Hubbell for their support and help in editing the manuscript; Janet Chappell for her assistance with the photos; and Anton Andy, Timothy Siebert, and William Skelton for their guidance relative to the content and format of the book.

Introduction

$\mathcal{M}$y brother and I are identical twins. All through school, no one could tell us apart; they just called us "the Chappell twins." We graduated from Ravenna Township High School in 1950 and worked for nearly a year in the A&P supermarket. The talk of all our fellow graduates was the Korean War and "who would get drafted." We were also helping our parents, Walter and Mildred Chappell, run a dairy farm on our sixty-acre Ravenna, Ohio, property and on an additional 145 acres in nearby Freedom.

Our chronicle (in the form of letters written to our parents) reports our exciting experiences during four years (March 1951–February 1955) in the military service. We were both prolific letter writers, and Mom saved every letter.

In 1998, we edited more than three hundred letters, condensing every three or four letters down to one in the process of deleting redundancies and idle talk—the weather, happenings at home, who sent cookies that never arrived, etc. Whenever we collapsed a number of letters into one—as, for example those of September 5, 9, and 11, 1952—we simply marked the letter with the last date (September 11, 1952).

Our story is typical of those of many Navy corpsmen who served with the Marine Corps. It is a serviceman-to-parent story that advances through varied assignments: boot camp; Hospital Corps School, U.S. Naval Hospital, and Fleet Marine Force training; duty in Korea on the front line, in battalion aid stations, and in the field medical hospital; and a tour in the Military Sea Transportation Service.

Gerald (Jerry), Walter (Dad), and Richard (Dick) Chappell before the boys
enlisted in the U.S. Navy

An introduction preceding the letters of each chapter gives background
on the Korean War generally. We have added some 1998 reflections at the end
of each chapter.

Our story actually begins a year before we entered the service. Dick and I
felt excitement and apprehension from the moment (June 27, 1950) that Pres.
Harry S Truman announced that the United States had entered the Korean
"police action," along with allies in the United Nations. Our government felt
it was important to stop the spread of communism into South Korea, and a
massive buildup of American forces was being fed by a military draft. From
that day throughout 1950, we followed with keen interest the war highlights
in Ravenna's *Evening Record,* Akron's *Beacon Journal,* and Cleveland's *Plain
Dealer.*

We had gone to work in the Ravenna A&P (which then stood for "Great
Atlantic and Pacific Tea Company") store early in 1950. Our weekday schedule, though, started before daylight—at 5 A.M., as we helped Dad milk by
hand our herd of fourteen dairy cows. It was on June 25 that the North Koreans, with the approval of China and the Soviet Union, attacked southward
across the thirty-eighth parallel. Soon afterward the United Nations Security
Council called for the assistance of all UN members in halting the invasion.

Ma Chappell standing
in front of the
farm garage

During most of Mom's delicious breakfasts of June–August, we listened to
the radio newscasters' updates on the war.

After breakfast we went to the A&P, where we were met by the manager,
Harrison Krupp. Dick, Harrison, and I had the first duty of the day, unloading the bread truck. We placed the large cartons full of loaves on carts and
wheeled them to shelves at the front of the store. The rest of the morning we
placed boxes and cans of goods on shelves.

We ate at noon with some coworkers (most frequently the assistant manager, George Christy, and a friend, Donald Baird) in a large room in the back
of the store. Then in the afternoon we opened boxes and stamped prices on
goods. The unbelievable events of the Korean War were our main focus of
discussion. Most of us knew very little about that faraway peninsula. Our
spirit was lifted when we heard on September 15 that troops commanded by
Gen. Douglas MacArthur had made a daring amphibious landing at Inchon,
far north of the main battlefront at Pusan. The convergence of UN forces
from the north and south had shattered the North Korean People's Army;

The Chappell farmhouse, near Ravenna, Ohio

more than 125,000 of the enemy had been captured. It was good news when MacArthur speculated that the American troops would be back home by Christmas.

After work, Dick and I always returned to the farm in time to help Dad milk the herd again. During the week, after a hearty meal prepared by Mom, we usually listened to a couple of radio programs and hit the sack. But on Friday or Saturday evenings, we picked up our old school buddies (most often Kenny Kline, Virgil Marsh, and Frank Leonard) in our Model-A Ford and went bowling or to a movie. We usually ended up hanging out at a favorite diner. The bleak war picture and our uncertain futures relative to it entered most discussions. By the end of November 1950, the newscasters and paper headlines were focusing on how the UN forces were boldly moving northward toward the Yalu River and the Manchurian border. Then, around Thanksgiving, 180,000 Chinese "volunteers" entered the war. By December 15, after bitter winter fighting and a harrowing retreat, the UN forces were driven back southward to the thirty-eighth parallel.

Having been movie buffs since elementary school, Dick and I were especially interested in war movies about the Marines; we had seen all those of the late forties. We followed all the headlines about the Marines and were aware that late in November 1950, months after the successful Inchon landing and the recapture of Seoul, MacArthur had sent the 5th and 7th Regiments of the First Marine Division, under the command of Gen. O. P. Smith, to the Chosin reservoir. Stories about the First Marine Division's hellish battle for and retreat from the Chosin reservoir were filtering back to the United States at the turn of the year. Word of such events encouraged us to enlist in the Navy, on March 5, 1951. We may have liked war movies, but we had no desire to become any form of combat soldier.

Chapter One

Boot Camp

To our parents' dismay, we were sent across the United States to "boot camp"—basic recruit training—in San Diego. This first set of letters describes our trials and tribulations.

The intense nature of boot camp kept us from dwelling upon the Korean War during our abbreviated, two-month training period. Still, we boot campers were aware of and concerned about some of the major events, as the newspapers focused upon them. For example, in April 1951 President Truman removed General MacArthur from command and replaced him with Gen. Matthew Ridgway. MacArthur had disagreed with the defense leaders in Washington about how the United Nations should conduct the war. While MacArthur had wanted to bomb bases in Manchuria, a part of China, and use other "all-out measures," Truman and his advisers feared such actions might lead to a third world war. Our boot camp reaction to MacArthur's dismissal was one of confusion, for the general opinion was that he was a sound leader. Ridgway went to Tokyo to replace MacArthur, and Lt. Gen. James A. Van Fleet became commander of the Eighth Army.

Letters

Hi Mom and Pop,   March 12, 1951

Hope you are both well. Frank, Jerry, and I all passed the Navy physical and have been traveling together ever since.

Someone sent us a clipping. Could be from our hometown Ravenna, Ohio, paper which you would have already seen, but I'm copying what it says for you just in case you haven't: "Three Ravenna Twp. high school graduates who recently enlisted in the Navy have been assigned to the San Diego, Calif., Naval Training Station for basic training. Richard George Chappell and Gerald Eugene Chappell, twin sons of Mr. and Mrs. Walter Chappell, Freedom Street, and Frank Bruno Leonard, son of Mr. and Mrs. William Leonard, 1206 W. Main Street, were sworn into Naval service recently. Gerald, an All–Portage County guard in football, and his brother were three-year letter winners at Ravenna Twp. Leonard also attended Kent State University."

We've traveled first class from Akron and I mean first class. Nine of us Navy fellows all rode in the best of Pullman cars right among some of the big business men of the country. We switched trains at St. Louis and took a coach train to Kansas City. After a nine-hour leave there, we took another Pullman and stopped in Denver for about two hours. Then we pulled into Salt Lake City (for being the capital of Utah, it's not too large), traveled through the desert and snow-capped mountains to Los Angeles, and arrived here in San Diego Saturday morning, March 10th. I saw some of the most picturesque mountain canyons I will probably ever see. The rock formations are really beautiful with all types and all colors. Saw cattle out grazing and horses running loose.

We received our Navy clothing this morning and our seabag, $254 dollars' worth. You should see us in sailor outfits. So far we've worn only our overalls and work shirts. We got our rifles and they are heavy. Looks like they do everything in a systematic order here. The base is much nicer than I anticipated it would be. Tonight we should go to a barracks where we will remain until after Boot Camp. Frank and six other men from Columbus plus the two of us will all have bunks together with the 83 men in our Company. We will have to scrub our own clothes on cement outside the barracks and keep them all in our seabag. The meals are large in quantity, but weak in flavor. Send your letters to Richard George Chappell, SR 571-80-61, Company 51-304, U.S. Navy Training Center, San Diego 33, Calif. Jerry's (571-80-62) is the same.

We have decided that we will take turns writing. Be good and have a good time while you are still young. And keep the dogs well fed.

Love, Dick

Dear Ma and Pa,   March 20, 1951

Seems like this is the first half hour I've had to myself since we got here.

In a fashion, this base is like the grounds of a college except many of the buildings are identical because they are company barracks. When a person looks around, he gets the impression that it's a clean military center. Between the barracks and buildings of more importance, there are long, smooth stretches of paved drilling space. The two-story barracks are built in an H shape and contain four companies each. You can rest assured that when I say these barracks are clean I mean just that. Two hours a day, one hour in the morning and one at night, we clean every inch of our section.

We had a Captain's Inspection this morning and everything had to be perfect. I'd swear we stood at attention, rotating with parade rest, for an hour and a half. For inspection, which is every morning, we have to have our work shirt pockets buttoned and empty. Nothing is allowed in our overalls' (dungarees') front pockets. Also, our undershirt (skivvies) and hats have to be clean and we have to be clean shaven with no side burns. For everything that isn't, a demerit is placed against our company.

We have the six classes to catch each day, three in the morning and three in the afternoon. We have already learned the Semaphore code and the 16-point manual (exercises done carrying the rifle). We do march to mess hall, wait in line for about an hour for a pretty good meal, and, after the meal, can stroll back to our barracks to fix our clothes, make our bunks, and get ready for inspection.

After we finish supper, we have to take a shower, shave, brush our teeth, shine our high shoes (boots), wash three or four pieces of clothes, roll up a couple of articles we didn't get done earlier, clean up a section of the compartment, fix our bed, and write a letter if we have time left. Taps blows at 9:30. The rest of the time depends on our Company Commander, Saunders. If we get what he wants done in good time and get in mess line, we eat earlier and have all evening. So far he seems to be a fair guy. If he doesn't like the way we do things, he can make us march Sat[urday] and Sun[day]. And there is a Recruit C.P.O. (Chief Petty Officer) whose name is Collier who tells us what to do about half the time. He takes over when the Commander isn't here. And there is an Assistant Recruit C.P.O., Barnes, who takes over when the C.P.O. isn't present.

There are some Alabama, Texas, and Georgia characters in our Company. I don't mind the marching, but I'm in front of some Alabama hillbilly who marches like he was chasing the cows over stones in a creek. He's always on my heels and never in step. Got to sign off for now.

Love, Jerry

Hi Mom and Pop   March 25, 1951

I got my picture taken and am sending it to you as an Easter present. If you are going to put any in the paper, please wait until we get some with our nice blue outfits on. It was really comical watching Frank open the box of goodies he got today (a lot of candy and cookies and three jars of pickles). It wasn't 10 minutes later that all but a few pickles were gone. Poor Jerry got there five minutes too late. I wonder who will get some goodies this afternoon that we can all eat (ha ha). Some of the fellows have received radios and others have guitars, so this place is beginning to sound like home.

Jerry and I found a method of making money when we have some extra time. Last night we made 75 cents and tonight 75 cents as well. We earn the money by rolling clothes. Everybody is supposed to roll their own clothes, but the Commander doesn't know the difference. Some guys will pay the 75 just for two pairs of pants which we can roll in about 10 minutes. We take the money we've earned to [the] Ship's Service [store] and buy goodies like ice cream and candy bars. Then we take the goodies back to our Company and sell them to the guys for twice as much. About 10 guys from the company buy Sunday papers and let the rest of us read theirs. Sometime this week we should learn what we did on our G.C.T. tests (General Classification Tests). Those results will mean very much.

Today we got another haircut. Cost 2 bits. Fifteen barbers shaved our 83 heads in about 15 minutes. I was in and out of the barber chair so fast I didn't have time to get my feet off the floor.

It's a good thing I'm back in shape, for I needed to be for a day like this. We started out at 7:00 this morning to be at Dental Six by 7:30. With Assistant Recruit C.P.O. Barnes in charge (who knows about as much about the place as the rest of us do), we started from our barracks near the center of the camp and went clear over to the northeast tip of the camp. Barnes decided it wasn't over there, brought us back near our camp, and took us clear over to the northwest tip. Barnes decided it wasn't there and brought us back past our barracks and across our drill field and there it was (about 9:00). I got one tooth filled and guess I'm all set. This afternoon it was drill, drill, drill. My legs and shoulders are sore as a result.

I took out $10,000 of life insurance and it's going to knock a hole in my monthly pay, about $19.30 a month. It's rather expensive, but at the end of 20 years I will be through paying insurance for the rest of my life. Jerry took out the same type, but only for $5,000.

They have good shows down here, like Mae West in person.

It seems like almost everyone we know around home has started out in some branch of service. We have yet to see our first drop of California rain.

How are the dogs and cows coming along? I hope you are all well and that you are not worrying about us. Just get out and enjoy life as if we were there.

Love, Dick

Dear Ma and Pa,   March 27, 1951

I want to wish you both a happy Easter. Thanks for your Easter cards and money. We also received a letter from Grampa and Grandma. It's good to hear from them and know that they are interested in what we are doing. We accidentally got sent to the wrong church yesterday and henceforth were Mormons. I've had very little trouble with my razor and seldom cut myself. It seems like all we do is go to classes. We had two on the birth of the American Navy, one on rates [enlisted ranks] and insignia, and three others that were on other Navy matters.

We had our first Regimental Drill early this morning. That's when we do our 16-point manual, semaphore, exercises, etc. with about six other companies. Only we do it to music under a director. If our personal and barracks inspection scores are high enough from now on, we do get to go to one movie a week by squads. Yesterday we played basketball with some of the Company and got blisters on our feet.

This boot camp holds a lot of fellows. We came in a week from last Sat. with our Company 304. Today I have seen companies up to 346, meaning that at the rate of 85 men to a company, that's more than 4,000 men in 11 days. Of course, earlier companies are graduating. I don't necessarily like the idea of washing clothes. And standing guard, I don't like even more. Two nights ago I had a night 12–2 patio watch (outside area where we wash our clothes) and tonight it's a 12–2 compartment watch (inside area where we sleep). Our system of keeping clothes all thrown together in our seabag is not very good. We try to keep one section that we seldom wear, another that we never wear (the rolled ones), and a third that we switch to every day. Wish we could at least have three bags within the seabag. All little incidentals such as our comb, shaving material, books and the like are kept in a ditty bag, separate from the seabag and hung on our bunk.

Our Company is divided into two different columns and each column is divided into three squads with about 12 men to a squad. Frank is in squad four. I'm in squad five, and Dick's in squad six. The squad that had the least points knocked off during the morning inspection got to go to the movie last night. Around five points are knocked off for things like a dirty undershirt or hat. You lose points for leggings folded wrong and buttons unbuttoned. Our Company Commander (about age 30) says our company hasn't been doing so well so we have had to march a lot.

We also had our first bag-layout practice. It's about the silliest thing I've ever done. All our rolled clothes, shaving equipment and everything we own have to be put in a certain position on our bunk. Next week it will count. If anything is not there or is out of place, we get marks against us.

Because enlistment in the Navy at this time is so heavy, the chances of us going to a school are very slim. The weather down here in California is almost perfect. The sun is bright but there is always a cool breeze.

Love, Jerry

Dear Ma and Pa,   April 10, 1951

We have gotten a few letters from Kenny Kline, and one from Virgil Marsh, Jim Hudson, and our A. and P. supermarket buddies Ronnie Newcome and Donald Baird. Kenny says he gets a lot of liberty and time off and thinks he will get to go to a school. As a Seaman Recruit we get $75 a month pay. He gets $70. In order to get out of Boot Camp, we have to pass our final achievement test, then we are Apprentice Seamen and our pay goes up to $82. There are about 25,000 guys in all the Navy Boot Camps, with nine to 10,000, or near full capacity, out here.

We finished our last week of primary. Here's a typical well-rounded day. We started out with personal inspection and our Company got a 3.72 [of a possible 4.00]. We proceeded to the swimming pool where we barely got a good dunking. That's because we have to take our leggings and boots off and then, naturally, put them back on (that is, unlace and lace everything). Next we had about an hour of drill which we don't mind now that the soreness is out of our bones. We have to carry our pieces (rifles) from one class to another. We then continued on to an hour class on the Navy in World War I. One boy was caught with a dirty hat at inspection, so he had to carry a bucket around all day to let it soak (ha ha). After eating a hearty dinner we filled in our I.D. cards and liberty cards. Boy you should see my picture for my I.D. card, for I'm sleeping as usual.

Our Company has moved to Camp Elliot Annex to start advanced training. Moving wasn't much fun, for we had to pack everything we own into our seabag, blankets and all. We got to ride about 20 miles in buses and see a little of California with our seabags following behind us in trucks. The houses are high up on cliffs, often surrounded by flowers. The highways are well planned so that you don't stop for stop lights and there are lots of underpasses and overpasses.

They have one long row of barracks here sitting on red dirt. We are on the bottom floor of our barracks and have much thicker mattresses. We hear all kinds of stories about the rattlers and Black Widow Spiders out here, but don't believe half of them. If we catch any snakes, we will send them home for pets (ha ha).

Dick and I have gotten into a very good deal. It's called Color Guard and consists of groups of three sailors who lead Brigades, Regiments, and Battal-

Sailors of a training unit marching in a dress parade

ions during our Dress Parades which all companies now participate in. We have the position of Staff men which is the one sailor of the group that salutes the Admiral as we pass him in the grandstand during a Dress Parade. Then each group also has a Leader who has a saber and gives the commands, and a Flag Bearer.

In a Dress Parade the Brigade Commander gives orders to the two Regiment leaders. Each Regimental Leader gives orders to five or six Battalion Leaders who then give orders to Company Commanders. It's complicated, but, when done properly, is really something to see. Saunders, our Company Commander, chose us to represent our Company in Color Guard. I'm not sure why. We get out of the morning personal inspections and bag layouts while we practice.

Love, Jerry

Hi Mom and Pop,   April 11, 1951

Wow, you bought a new Buick! That's really getting up in style.

Are the milking machines causing any trouble? Thanks for the great goodie boxes we got from you and both grandmas. Frank got a letter from our classmate Dave Green who's in the Coast Guard.

The different squads just switched cleanup duty today and all I have to do is sweep the dust off of five screens. That's easy compared to washing and polishing the metal work on the sinks.

We had our classification interviews today and our grades were as follows: Jerry: 58 (General) 55 (Math) 47 (Mechanical) and 54 (Clerical); Dick: 52, 52,

47 and 58. Of our whole company, there were about 35 above me and 45 below, putting me over average. We both put in for Radio School (needed a combination of 110 on the first and last score), but they told us our chances were slim. Because of the large number of guys here and the stiffness of the competition, even those with 60 averages probably won't get to go to any school. Jerry put in for Electrician School as his 2nd choice which was a bit high for me. Since my scores were good enough, the sailor interviewing me suggested I put down Hospital Division because it does include going to school on the East Coast. Frank had a 65 average and was one of the top five. They put him down for Personnel and Yeoman School.

Frank, Dick, and I had our first 12-hour liberty a couple of days ago. We took the bus directly from Camp Elliott with a round trip price of 45 cents. Left camp at 1300 and returned to it at 0100. Spent most of the afternoon looking over San Diego. It's not a large town and doesn't take much time to look over. Everywhere you go you see sailors. After getting something to eat, we went bowling. I enjoyed playing and got better each game, ending with a score of 137.

Love, Dick

Hi Mom and Pop, April 25, 1951

We received more candy from you and were sure tickled to get it. It was all in one piece and not smashed one bit. Well, we get paid tomorrow and I get 50 bucks. Jerry is getting $55. I plan to put $60 in the Saving Depository at N.T.C. Besides getting paid, we'll be leaving Camp Elliott.

Well, our Company started a week of Galley duty last night and went into full swing today. We miss that with our regular two periods of Color Guard a day, our compartment cleanups in the morning, and now about two hours of watch a day. Frank has to participate. His job is a tray washer. He really enjoys it (ha ha).

Today they started making us wear big belts to carry bullets and they claim that down at the other base they have started wearing helmets. The Company had a bagroll inspection a couple days ago and guess what we got—a 2.67. I'll bet that is the lowest score this base has ever had. Neither Jerry nor I were in it—Lucky!

However, we didn't miss the last bag inspection yesterday. I pulled a 4.00, but Jerry had several mistakes and got a 3.97. He had the heads on a couple of knots that go around his rolled pants pointing in the wrong direction (ha ha).

I finished my 5th day on the rifle range. The first two days we didn't do any shooting. Just worked with our straps to learn our positions and sighting.

Then the demonstrations with pistols and machine guns were quite interesting. Finally got to shoot 36 rounds with a .22 rifle and 40 rounds with the M-1 (.30 caliber) rifle (using four different positions). My score of 141 is about average and above qualifying at 130. I am glad I finished up, because it's been raining all day and who wants to wallow in the mud.

I finally participated in the Regimental Dress Parade last Saturday. It was rather hot and quite a few fellows passed out. The first thing you usually hear is a gun hitting the deck, and then the sailor. The two closest guys to them carry them off the field.

With a liberty coming up, I got so low on money I had to buy some candy bars and sell them for double the price. Have also been "taking in" and washing other guys' clothes to make money. Unfortunately, because I do such a fast job of washing my own, they are beginning to look a little grimy.

On my liberty I went into San Diego, got something to eat, and caught the bus for Balboa Park. It's a large zoo with plenty to see. We have been having some interesting classes lately covering the History of the U.S. Navy, sex (or how to avoid getting in trouble with bad women), first aid, and advancements in rank.

How is the painting on the house coming and the work on repairing the barn?

Love, Dick

Dear Ma and Pa,   May 5, 1951

Hope Mother had a great birthday!

Well, we finally landed back in barracks 53 in the main camp and got back on schedule this morning. It was interesting. We had talks on the different parts of a boat and got to row the small 13-men rowboats.

It's true, we only have to have nine weeks total of boot training. That's amazing because the companies that are now forming (around number 475) have 14 weeks. Our last week will start Thursday the 10th, and, if everything goes right, we will be leaving for home about the 17th. Before we come home, we should know what our orders are (either school or sea duty). If we don't pass our final achievement test, we may not be home until June. I am worried, because they say it's plenty rugged.

Guess it's a good thing we are about done. Our Company pulled a 2.99 on barracks inspection so naturally Saunders was quite peeved. Mainly because he has to go to classes every night this week for two hours as a result, I guess to become a better commander.

We had our Seaman's test, which is hardly a test in that it's a preparatory review for our final achievement test.

The guys from our Company that are working Galley duty (Including Frank) are working their heads off. They start about 4:30 in the morning and get through about 7:00.

Dick and I, being in the Color Guard, were put on a barracks cleanup with five other guys. Our daily schedule varies but is something like this: Get up at 4:30 and clean up the barracks, eat and go to Color Guard at 7:30 until 9:00, have the rest of morning off unless on watch (have one two and ½ hour watch a day), eat and go back to Color Guard until two, and have afternoon off until supper. We have only about one night watch a week (patio watch is not needed when the Company is working Galley). The other evenings are free. I went to a movie Wed. and Thurs. night and might go back again to-night. (Some fun, huh?)

Now that we are in our 8th week they really clamp down on us. Most of the offenses are up to 50 demerits (10 hours on the grinder). Some of them include not mustering, spitting on the deck, smoking when the light is out, and not getting up at a reveille. Last night 20 of the Company went on the grinder for two hours for having dirty towels on their bunks. After two hours, the only thing they wanted to do was hit the sack. Then came a bigger blow. They had a muster for our platoon for clean up duty and a mess of them were not here. I pity those guys for getting 50 demerits. I just happened to be here myself, for I'm usually at the movies or Ship's Service. When we have a fire drill, everybody has to get out of the barracks fast. Well a lot of fellows were caught with just their shorts on last night. One guy lost his shorts and had to run around for about half an hour with nothing on but his birthday suit. It must be getting warmer back there if Dad can start plowing.

Love, Jerry

Hi Mom and Pop,   May 15, 1951

All the news is good news. All three of us passed our final achievement test. Frank (the rascal) had to go and get the high score as usual. High for the Company that is. There were 12 from our Company that failed the final test. They are a sick looking group. About nine are going to be put back two weeks and will be given another chance to pass the test. Should they fail three times, they will be sent to sea without leave.

Jerry is getting $60 pay this time and I am getting $55, plenty enough money to get us home from Maryland. We are both definitely going to Maryland for Hospital School. When we first got our orders, they had Jerry coming back here to San Diego unassigned. Probably would have ended up out to sea painting decks. Well, we went to talk to Saunders, saying we were sure disappointed that we were going to be split up. He was sympathetic and sent us over to the Classification Office to see what we could work out. As a result, we ended up in some big shot base Commander's office. He gave us two choices: 1, Go to sea duty (a ship) together, or 2, Go to Hospital School together. Well we jumped on the second choice and he just scribbled in a change of orders for Jerry.

Now to make things complicated, when we were first classified according to orders, if we had a one in back of our name it meant taking our leave from here. If we had a zero in back of our names we would take our boot leave after we got to our next post. That is, the government would pay for our transportation to the next post. If the leave is from Maryland, it means 10 or 11 days at home rather than six or seven from way out here. Because Jerry's was originally a one, and because we made the request that he go to Hospital School at a later date, it may mean that he will have to take his boot leave from here and then when he gets back he will be sent to Bainbridge, Maryland. If, however, the act of changing orders can straighten everything out by the time we leave for home, then he also may go first to Bainbridge and then home. Jerry ordered bus tickets to Akron just in case he gets his leave from here.

Well, two things that you wanted are coming true. Namely, that we are being sent to a base that is a great deal closer home and that we are getting a shore school rather than sea duty. We don't necessarily like the idea of studying medicine, but both agreed it would be better than no school at all. It will take me five days by train to get to Maryland and another to get home.

Glad to hear that you and Mrs. Leonard are getting well acquainted. Just hope that the two of you don't get together and bawl during your visits.

The Company got together and gave Commander Saunders a gift of $100 ($1.25 apiece).

Frank, Dick and I took off for Mission Beach Sunday after attending church. It's a nice beach, but the amusement park isn't worth much. Since we didn't care to swim, we soon headed back for San Diego. Saw a release movie we had seen years ago, *The Fighting Sullivans.*

Went to see a movie last night, and liked it (*You're in the Navy Now*). New York sure won an easy victory over the Indians yesterday. Also Joe Louis. Glad to hear that Dad got some oats planted. Got to go for now, because if I don't, I'll be writing in the dark.

Love, Dick

Dear Ma and Pa,   May 17, 1951

The last couple of days we have had a lot of fun. We got the final test off our minds and have been having mostly films in our classes. We were Staff men in our last Dress Parade and rather enjoyed it. Only two of our Company that failed have been put back. The poor boys who have to go clear home for leave and then come back here have already bought their tickets. Frank has to come back here unassigned. He should be home sometime soon.

I just got back from the disbursing office and what do you think they are going to do to me? I was never so shocked in my life. After requesting the Hospital School weeks after the others, I thought I would have to stick around here for the next draft. But the old Navy came through and gave me my orders. I am to report to the Bainbridge Naval Hospital base in five days (the 22nd) to take my leave from there. That's only about 350 miles from home (a stone's throw). They are only giving me $176.64 to get there with (ha ha). In other words, I could take a bus and have $100 left over, if I wanted to. Dick will probably go by train, so I think I will try to catch the same one.

Love, Jerry

Dear Ma and Pa,   May 23, 1951

I arrived in Baltimore on Schedule and could have left here for home, but am waiting for Dick to show up this afternoon. Because I was sent by special orders, I got away from N.T.C. on Thursday. The word is that Dick's travel draft (group), which included 50 guys headed for Bainbridge, were held up until Saturday. I guess when they went to the train station someone stole a wallet and they postponed the trip waiting for the thief to bring it forward. Guess he never did, and they finally let the draft travel. See you at home soon.

Love, Jerry

Reflections

DICK: My attitude about enlisting was positive. I viewed joining the Navy as a great opportunity to "see the world." There was no fear, no concern, and the spirit of adventure was strong. Raised on the farm, we were physically fit and ready for whatever boot camp had to throw at us. When the Navy roused us out of bed at 0500, it wasn't much different from getting up to milk the cows. Adjusting to mess hall food, the rigorous pace of training, and the lack of personal privacy didn't bother us.

At first the Navy Way of managing clothing (wrapping, packing, and storing everything neatly in seabags) seemed overdone and silly, but it soon became clear that it was all part of the drill. Why not learn to march, handle weapons, and work in a cohesive unit? When it was all done, we viewed boot camp as a "fun" experience we were proud to have completed.

Swabbies Jerry and Dick home on leave following boot camp, standing next to the granary

JERRY: When I entered the Navy, and especially boot camp, I looked forward to the challenge. I had read Joseph Conrad's stories about a young man who experienced, coped with, and survived a series of adventures and became a better man. Confident, I too wanted to "test the stuff of which I was made." My education in the Ravenna Township School System had been a good one, and I had performed competitively on football and track teams of championship quality. Also, my folks had given me the wealth of insights inherent in a good, healthy farm life.

The real (smiling)
Commander Saunders

When Dick and I announced to the manager (Harrison Krupp) of the A&P where we were working at the time that we had enlisted in the Navy, his parting remark was something like, "I know you boys will do well. In all my years of managing a store, I have never seen an employee that could match your strong dawn-to-dusk work ethics."

I do have to remark further about the "little PX racket" that Dick and I had in boot camp. Because we were in the Color Guard, we had a freedom of movement (around our times of practice) none of the other trainees had. While they were spending hours marching and holding inspections, we could stand in line at the PX to buy ditty bags full of candy bars, cigarettes, and other choice purchases. Then, of course, we sold all those valued goodies back at the barracks for a substantial profit.

I smile when I recall our company commander, Saunders, for he was quite different from my image of what a "commander" should be. He was a rough,

Boot camp, Company 304. Frank Leonard is third from the right side in the front row, Jerry is second from the left in the third row, and Dick is second from the right in the back row.

salty swabbie, a 3rd-class petty officer whose foul mouth at first shocked us innocent Ohio farm boys. A tough disciplinarian with a stinging bark, he marched us until we were ready to drop, taught us which was our right foot and which was left in a hurry (and surprisingly, this was a major accomplishment for some of the recruits), and made us regret any "goofing up" on an inspection.

Saunders would move through the barracks around 0500 rattling our bunks with some blunt object, yelling something like "Come on you useless goddamned swabbies. Let go of your cocks, grab your socks, and hit the deck. We are moving your sorry asses out of here!" Even his cadence calls during marching drills would have shocked dear old Mom and Dad.

But he was just part of the test, and he did it well, covering a heart of gold with a posture of gruffness. We graduated from boot camp feeling we had met the challenge, and we thought fondly of our commander and his part in that success story. We had not yet found our manhood, but we had a good start.

Chapter Two

Hospital Corps Training School

So off we flew from one coast to the other to learn how to be hospitalmen. We waved as we flew over the Ohio farm fields. This second set of letters covers our five-month period of study at Hospital Corps School. Dick and I were "gung ho" to lead our classes in grades, because we knew the top graduates would get first choice for hospital placement. We also knew that a good academic record might lead to additional schooling. So we hit the books and put our excellent short-term memories to work, learning endless facts (nursing through anatomy) that later were about as useful as a hill of beans. We weren't sure we were cut out to be male nurses, but we liked the fact that naval personnel of the United States of America were going to take a crack at further educating us. We did prove that we could apply ourselves and succeed academically.

During the early months (June and July) we were at Bainbridge, the East Coast papers reported that it was a relatively quiet period in Korea, because of the truce talks and unusually heavy rain. However, at the end of July the Eighth Army, which included the First Marine Division, had to fight north of the thirty-eighth parallel around a circular valley known as the Punchbowl. The North Koreans had commanded the hills that rose sharply to heights of one to two thousand feet around the Punchbowl on the west, north, and east. From those positions they had easily observed, and directed artillery fire at, UN defenses and troop movements. So General Van Fleet used the Eighth Army to probe those Communist defenses, determine the disposition of their troops, and prevent them from employing their mounting offensive capabilities.

During August, the UN forces engaged in the battles of Bloody Ridge and Heartbreak Ridge. The statistics were not encouraging. The Korean War had already resulted in over a million military casualties (killed, wounded, or captured UN and Communist soldiers). Two million civilians had died, and three million more had been made homeless. The North Korean military adventure had failed, as had the UN attempt to impose a military solution and the Chinese attempt to force the UN out of Korea. There was some good news—the Soviet Union, seeing the failure that had befallen first the North Koreans and then the Chinese, had proposed truce talks.

In September the North Koreans, weakened by heavy losses, finally evacuated their positions. After almost three weeks of fighting and over 2,700 UN and Republic of Korea casualties, the Eighth Army won its objective.

Dick and I, and all our fellow sailors in training, tried to make light of the war reports, but deep inside us such news was most worrisome.

Letters

Hi Folks,   June 21, 1951

We hope Dad had a happy "Fathers Day."

We are officially students in the 19th class to be formed! That puts us among the 1000 students now enrolled. Our address is Richard G. Chappell SA and Gerald E. Chappell SA Class No. 19 U.S.N.H.C.S., N.H. Bainbridge, Md. It is just as simple as that. Pass it on to the rest of the people, and, if you want to, put it in the paper.

We have had three days of classes including Anatomy and Physiology (Mr. Harris), Nursing (Miss Stafford), Minor Surgery and First Aid (Occhipinti), Pharmacy (Mr. Evans), and Chemistry. They really pour the stuff at us. Most of the words are big too. Pages of notes have already accumulated. I can see right now that we'll be kept plenty busy with studies.

About every day they add some more rules, and, if it keeps up, we will not have any freedom. We only have five minutes between classes and can't get much writing done there. If we didn't have to go and wait in chow line it might be different, for that takes up about three hours a day of our free time.

Yesterday was a good example of a routine day. First, we had a two-hour class in Nursing of which the teacher spent most of the time teaching us how to make a bed (we practiced and both got graded a "very good"). Then two hours of Chemistry. I can see now that if a person had not had any previous chemistry, it would be over his head. Then three hours of Hygiene and Sanitation. Took about four pages of notes in all. In the last hour period, First Aid and Minor Surgery, Mr. Occhipinti sprung a surprise test on us. Both got a 90 percent.

Tomorrow we will go through our first Friday Inspection. I have been pressing my clothes. Most of the time we don't get done all that we planned to in an evening. For instance, if we wash, that's all we can do. If we don't have anything but studies, we can usually work in the movies. If there are letters to write, we either drop the movies or studies. The movies are usually old and we either have or haven't seen them. The nights that we have seen the show we do one of the other things (get me?).

Finally received letters from Kenny Kline and Virgil Marsh. It is good to hear that Aunt Dell has arrived from Pontiac for her annual summer visit.

We are on Duty Section 4, which means every fourth night, 4th Wednesday, and 4th weekend we have duty.

The best classes in inspection tomorrow will get to eat first for the next week.

Love, Dick

Dear Ma and Pa,   July 26, 1951

We've received letters from you folks, Jim Hudson, Bruce Patterson, Skip Maur, the Hills, the Dudaks, and Grampa and Grandma Chappell.

In Nursing we have just finished bed baths (Both got a "very good"). Dick's couldn't have been too bad, because his patient was sound asleep most of the time. When we get home, we will teach you how to take the bottom sheet off and put it on the top or another clean sheet on the bottom, so that in the future you can change our beds while we keep right on sleeping (ha ha). Monday we start into blood pressure and pulse rates. One chap in our class isn't too smart and all the teachers pick on him all the time. Another Brooklyn boy can get into trouble without moving his finger. We had that tough test in Pharmacy that everybody was worrying about. Because Dick was going to sick bay last week with a virus, he asked Mr. Fisher, our teacher, if he could take the test the period before he went. Well, it seems that he was a guinea pig. The teacher had two different tests he could give us, and according to the grade Dick got, he would determine if he should give that test or the other. I don't know what the other one was like, but it couldn't have been

Jerry and Dick in their casual dark-blue naval outfits

any tougher. Well, somehow Dick got about a 96 percent on it, so the rest of the class got stuck with that test. I really messed up on mine (88 percent).

Dick may not be able to get out of sickbay to come home this weekend, but I will make the trip. Expect to get home sometime between 7:30 and 9:30.

Love, Jerry

Hi Mom and Pop,   August 7, 1951

Well guess what? We had a wonderful weekend in New York City! Ronnie Stellwag, a boy in Jerry's class, who lives near New York City, invited us up for the weekend. The three of us took off from Perryville by train at 12:00 noon and arrived about 3:30 in New York.

Our New York host,
Ronnie Stellwag

Saw the Empire State Building (went up to the 86th floor) and the famous Belmont Race Track, swam at Jones Beach, and took in Times Square. In the evening we rode the subway and saw a good stage and movie combination: Danny Lester, the Martiniers, Bob Chester and his band plus the latest Jerry Lewis and Dean Martin picture. Ronnie has a wonderful family that showed great hospitality.

Guess what else? I finally got back from sickbay to attend classes several days last week. Only it's Class 20. Being that my notes were up with class 19, this week will be just a review. The composition of Class 20 looks a lot like 19, meaning a lot of the boys are smart and about ten have had college experience.

I will bring you up to date on some of the others as time passes on.

Love, Dick

Dear Ma and Pa,   August 21, 1951

Our shots are finally over and I'm glad of it, because I don't make such a good shooter. Our needle for the buttocks is an inch and a half long. I bent the first one.

After studying about tetanus (disease located in manure and found around presence of animals which is transferred into the body by stepping on a nail), I'm beginning to think we are lucky for not getting it, because I don't know how many times we have stepped on nails in our life. If the disease is transferred, it will cause lockjaw and one of the most agonizing deaths possible. However, if the tetanus antitoxin shot is taken within so many hours, it will kill the bacteria. So if you hear of any kids stepping on a nail, make sure they get the shot. We are studying appendicitis, gall stones, etc. in Minor Surgery.

We've also been discussing transfusions. They use two and ½ to 3-inch needles for that. A good thing we don't have to give them.

Bacteriology is different and fairly interesting. We have been looking at Gonococcus—Streptococcus and Staphylococcus on slides. The microscopes are quite expensive and good ones. Today I managed to apprehend a small creature hardly visible to the eyes and examine it. Much fun. We have also seen a film on poisonous gases that was interesting.

Love, Jerry

Hi Mom and Pop,   September 27, 1951

I have given and been given my 1st shot. The whole thing was rather amusing. There is only one colored boy in my class and somehow I got stuck with him. He gets very nervous every time he sees a needle. The nurse had to hold him down while I stuck it in. Then, somehow with the Nurse telling him every step, he finally gave it to me.

Frank has arrived at his new station in San Francisco. I guess by the way he tells it, he has really got it made. He doesn't have to be to work until 8:30. He only works two days out of a week and has liberty all the rest of the time (sounds fishy). With that kind of set up, the poor boy will never be able to save any money.

Love, Dick

Hi Mom and Pop,   October 24, 1951

HAPPY BIRTHDAY DAD!

Let's see, that makes you what? 32? We hope you enjoyed the present even though we were not there. Everything is closed up here this weekend, so we couldn't even buy a card.

We are studying cancer and lumbar punctures in Nursing. In MSFA [Minor Surgery and First Aid] we are doing what is known as field problems. Although we have been using the auditorium, we are supposed to have a case out on the field. Yesterday I had a chap with a simple fractured tibia. It's good practice.

Jerry's teacher, Miss Stafford, said the other day that she had 200 questions all ready for the Nursing final and wasn't finished making out the test. It

Jerry with naval buddy Bobby G. Day

is rumored that we may graduate on the 10th or on the 15th of November. Let's hope it's the 15th to put us home on leave for Thanksgiving.

Love, Dick

Hi Mom and Pop,   November 7, 1951

I don't know whether Jerry wrote to you over the weekend or not, but here is the latest dope on current events. First Jerry, Bobby Day, Donald Beck and five other boys from Class 19 got Bethesda [Naval Hospital, at the Naval Medical Center, Bethesda, Maryland, outside Washington, D.C.]. Castro was the Class 19 Honor man with a 97.5 percent average (Jerry had 97.4 percent). Duke is going to Annapolis, Md. It is now Friday night and I am the proud owner of a 97.55 percent average. I got Bethesda even though I was sixth in choosing it. There were 10 others from class 20–21 that picked it after me. With the three classes combined they are sending 21 boys down to Bethesda Naval Hospital. Kyser from my class took Honor man with a final average of 98.016 percent. A boy from another class by the name of Hedges took first with a final average of 98.75 percent. I'm not sure, but I believe that is the second highest score that has come out of this school.

The two of us were in the upper six from all three classes combined.

Monday and today I was working in ward 819. It's an Orthopedics ward and deals mostly with osteology cases which concerns broken bones. I gave T.P.R.'s [temperature, pressure, and repiration checks] and worked on the book work some plus running errands.

You had better dig our clothes out. We will be needing them over the 10-day leave. You better not write back because chances are we would never get it.

Love, Dick

Dear Ma and Pa,   November 9 , 1951

I've worked in O.R. (Operating Room). Watched a circumcision which was interesting. Saw them use an electric cauterizing machine on several warts. They also took a large fatty tumor out of some chap's leg. I helped wrap rubber gloves and swab down the operating room. Also witnessed two herniaplasties and the removal of a pellionella cyst. Both of the herniaplasties were painless because a spinal anesthetic was used. The days went by very fast.

Thurs. we were all switched around again, so I ended up in the Blood Bank as one of the prep men. My job was to get the sailors who were donating into position, get the tourniquet around their arm (so that it could be tightened), and prepare the area so that it was surgically clean (soap, alcohol and Iodine), etc. Although we work from nine to one, all we do in the afternoon is clean up and prepare for the next morning. Tomorrow I will see how the Surgery Ward is run where the patients are prepared for the operations.

Graduation is definitely set for the 10th for all—Too Bad! We won't be home for Thanksgiving.

Our Anatomy and Physiology final was to name all 206 bones, and describe the digestive system and the respiratory system. My Nursing final was over everything (about 175 questions).

Looks like I will be heading for the Bethesda Hospital. Also Don Beck and Bobby Day. There were very few southern openings so most of the southern chaps are staying north.

Training School buddies Charles Duke and Donald Beck

When we get home, you know we like cider that is about a week old with a nice bite to it. Some cinnamon rolls would taste good. Hope the new milk house hasn't changed the place so much that we don't recognize it.

My class gets its picture taken tomorrow morning.

Love, Jerry

Reflections

JERRY: One other life experience and lesson sticks in my mind. It happened one warm, sunny afternoon when a group of us students were lying around

U.S. Naval Hospital Corps School Class 19–51

in the grass outside our barracks. Perhaps it was a Sunday, and we were just relaxing and chewing the fat.

One of the students, Jerry Rollins, tended to be argumentative with anyone he could sucker in. He continually bragged about being the best at doing everything. On that afternoon his claim was that he could out-armwrestle anybody, so a number of students accepted his challenge, including me. I'm not sure who won my match, but my guess is that he let me win that round. However, he was soon betting that no one could outwrestle him and make him say "uncle."

Well, Dick and I had wrestled with each other all the way through school and we thought we were quite tough. In addition, Rollins was a skinny little shrimp who weighed only about a hundred pounds (we were both about 160). So I was quick to volunteer to take him on, thinking it would be as easy as eating cherry pie to make the little guy say "uncle." But Dick also volunteered, perhaps with a little greater wager.

As a number of students placed their bets, Rollins went through the "eeeny, meeny, miney, moe" jingle and selected Dick. Well, it turned out to be a great wrestling match. It seemed to go on forever, but it ended with the little shrimp making Dick croak out a muffled "uncle." Afterward I thanked the Lord that I had escaped that little tussle. I figured Rollins had been on his high school wrestling team and was some kind of state champion, maybe lightweight division. He had, probably from the start, hustled us Ohio farm boys, setting us up for a fall. I did learn two lessons from the experience: watch out for hustlers in life, and realize you can't always tell the strength and skill of another person merely by looking at his or her size and physique.

As we headed for duty near the capital of our nation, I saw myself as a potential male Florence Nightingale, and my spirits were high.

DICK: Although Jerry's tale of my wrestling match suggests that we had a combative nature, I've always viewed the two of us as very easy to get along with. Many of the guys in boot camp and training school (and in follow-up assignments) were attracted to us as twins and by our friendly Ohio acceptance of people. We loved finding out where guys we met came from, and we liked kidding them about aspects of their states differing from the merits of good old Ohio. There was something thrilling, rich, and rewarding about getting to know fellows from all over the country. (Thirty-one states were represented in our two hospital training classes, and perhaps the rest of the states in boot camp. See the appendix for the class lists.) Some of the friendships we cultivated at Bainbridge matured in later duty stations.

When Jerry and I heard about the bloodshed occurring in Korea in fights such as those of Bloody Ridge (its defense alone cost the enemy over fifteen thousand casualties) and Heartbreak Ridge, we were glad our service assignment was going to be in a nice, clean, safe naval hospital. I do not recall that we yet knew, at this point, that the Marine Corps traditionally called upon the Navy's hospitalmen to take care of its wounded in battle.

Chapter Three

Bethesda Naval Hospital

$\mathcal{T}$he letters of this chapter tell about our seven-and-a-half-month experience in our first duty post—the Navy's finest hospital, in Bethesda, Maryland. The doctors and nurses were the best the service could muster, and many of our patients were high-level military or political figures. As comfortable as we felt within the confines of the tour of duty at the Bethesda Naval Hospital, there was always an uneasiness about how long we would remain there. The military grapevine generally kept us informed about the status of things in Korea. We heard that the war had become positional—that is, our troops and the enemy's troops were dug in, skirmishing with each other on a main line of resistance.

The Korean positional war was like a throwback to the western front of World War I rather than a successor to World War II, in the static quality of the battlefield, the defense in depth with its barbed wire and intricate series of trenches, the accent on artillery and mortar fire, and the everlasting patrols and raids. No matter how cautious the commanders were in risking lives, enemy artillery and mortar fire often found their targets, and enemy ambushes and probes caused the list of dead and wounded to mount. The fact that there was deadlock at the truce negotiations at Panmunjom and stalemate at the front was not encouraging.

Letters

Dear Mom and Pop,   December 13, 1951

The meals have been excellent! Much better than at Camp Bainbridge.

The Hospital has a big gym for the corpsmen with a large swimming pool, a basketball floor, a bowling alley and a pool room. We've been over there a lot and it's really nice. I'm getting very good at keeping score in bowling and my average is up to 115. They have a great movie theater and a big library that should provide any type of reference we may need.

I finally got assigned to the Neurosurgical Ward (6-C) which has around 43 patients and deals with problems of the nervous system. Some are paraplegics (paralyzed legs) due to an accident or some other means.

We are both on P.M. care and were lucky enough to be on the same shift as Bobby Day and Don Beck. Jerry is up in Tower 12.

One fellow we just admitted has nerve trouble in the brain and frankly I believe he should be up stairs in the Psychiatric Ward. I like the ward and on my shift I work with two other corpsmen whom both seem like good joes. We are not too busy, but have enough to do to keep it from being boring. Three fellows were sent up to the x-ray room where a spinal tap removed some of the cerebrospinal fluid from their spinal canal. Two needles were forced into the lumbar region between the 2nd and 5th lumbar vertebras. As the fluid drained from the lower needle, they forced air into the upper. The air travels up the spinal column and enters the brain. Well after taking the patients up and bringing them back, I had to record and take all cardinal symptoms (T.P.R.s and blood pressure) every 15 minutes on all three patients.

I have one very nice nurse on my ward and one that isn't quite so nice. For an overall opinion of the ward, I like it. Yesterday I gave my first shot on it to a colored boy (as usual). Our morning time goes fast when we eat two meals, shower and shave, run around for this thing or another and muster now and then. I will probably start as the galley corpsman for my ward and will serve the food to the patients.

Bobby Day, who got here about a week before we did, got put on the Dependents Ward and due to the fact it contains mostly women, he has a rather easy job of it. Donald Beck on the other hand, is on a ward with mostly old admirals and it keeps him jumping. One of the boys, George Karos, got a special watch the other night and the Brigadier General that he was watching passed away. Nothing like having your first patient die, is there?

My correct address is Richard G. Chappell, H.A., [Hospitalman Apprentice] N.N.M.C., Building 12, Bethesda 14, Md. The N.N.M.C. stands for National Naval Medical Center.

Love, Dick

Dear Ma and Pa,   December 17, 1951

Well things are going really good. I am up on Tower 12 which is one of the major Surgical Wards. Each floor in the main building is called a Tower. We have a total capacity of 18 beds. At present there are only nine beds occupied. Most of the patients are ambulatory and can go down to chow hall to eat during the A.M. shift. A chow cart comes up the elevator for the others. You have to work like a mad man before Friday inspections, sweeping, swabbing, dusting, waxing, and buffing 12 rooms. We do have buffing machines that really knock off the hard labor. I'm also chief silverware washer (sterling silver) but don't have to wash any dishes, because I just send them back on the cart. One of my doctors pulled a tube out of a patient's chest that was supposed to be drawing out excess blood, but wasn't. So the doc got surprised by a bed full of blood.

Our patients are several Lieutenants, a post-operation Captain, about three Lt. Cols., one Commander, a couple of Marine Majors, and an Admiral. The admiral is doing pretty well, although he is our most stubborn patient. Today two operations were scheduled, a thyroidectomy and a hernia repair so things should start picking up.

Last week the Hospital had all kinds of entertainment lined up, including Charlie McCarthy and Edgar Bergen and Blackstone the Magician. Good shows. Dick and I were both surprised to see that we passed the Hospital Corpsmen's Test along with Bobby Day. It's a tough test and quite a few of the guys failed and will have to take it the next time.

Since we will probably not have another liberty until New Year's, we really made a weekend out of the past one. Friday the snow hit us with about 4 inches.

Oh, I almost forgot, we met a Cleveland chap who is leaving for sea duty late this month. He has a '41 Plymouth and has just overhauled the motor. The body and paint job are good for the age of the car and it looks and sounds good. He let us borrow the Plymouth, if we filled it with antifreeze. It was so bad out that cars were sliding all over. It took us about an hour to get into Bethesda. Once the streets were bare, we took off for Washington D.C. with Beck, Williams, and Day and met Duke at his hotel for a weekend reunion. We visited the Health Museum (Which we found right down our line

Jerry in blues, Dick in whites, in front of the Bethesda Naval Medical Center

and very interesting), tried several restaurants, took in a movie, then drove down to Alexandria to give it the once over. They have Xmas trees all over and it really looks nice. D.C. is really well decorated. We came back to base, bowled and played some basketball, found Duke a rack [bunk] to sleep in, and got up Sunday morning and all went over to the Protestant Church for services. Now what we want you to do is send a money order for $125 to each of us as soon as you can. He wants $200 for the car, and, with Xmas shopping and all, we will need that much more. This morning I am going to see if I can get the car signed over.

I haven't started Xmas shopping yet. My three Bendixes of wash just got through, so I will hang everything up.

Love, Jerry

Dear Ma and Pa,   December 24, 1951

Hope you are having a Merry Xmas. I am on duty tonight and as we approach the Xmas holiday we have only one patient, a Vice Admiral who was in an automobile accident the other day. There are two of us (myself and Colley) to feed one meal, take one T.P.R., and do a little cleaning for the next few days. Tonight we had to give several medications, do a little dusting and shine some brass, and the rest of the time we sit around.

You probably know we got two packages of nuts and candy from Uncle Frank and Aunt Lila and one package of cookies from Grandma Richardson. As each patient checked out for Xmas, they left a box of candy, so we have boxes stacked all over the place. Don't mind having the duty over Xmas but sure am glad I have leave scheduled for over New Year's.

They keep our refrigerator filled with orange juice, chocolate milk, and plain milk for the patients, and us, to drink.

Love, Jerry

Hi Mom and Pop,   December 26, 1951

Happy Holidays! It is now afternoon and things are running so slowly I can write a letter on ward duty. We are putting in 14 hours of work every day over the Xmas holiday. We usually have around 45 patients, but because of the Holidays we only have 10. Since I've been on galley, all I've done is eat, eat, and eat more.

Last week we were out about every night, often with Don Beck, and Bobby Day. Took in a Spanish dancing outfit that was very enjoyable (sat clear up in the 2nd balcony, but could still see okay), saw the movie "Quo Vadis" in D.C., hit a good stage show, and went skating twice (to my surprise I could still maneuver my feet).

Last night for entertainment a couple of good-looking Hula Dancers came in from some big club in D.C. When Charlie McCarthy was here, he spent most of his time flirting with Miss Stoops who is our good-looking 25 year young nurse.

Got the car inspected by the Hospital Inspection Party to allow us in and out of the gate without any trouble to worry about. As far as the progress on the car goes, it's slow but sure. We had to buy two new tires for the Plymouth. Cost $15 apiece, so if you want to really send us a good birthday present you can send enough money to pay for one of them. We now own it, have it registered, and got the Ohio plates on (16 bucks for the Ohio tags). It cost $10 to get the front wheels straightened and balanced. Looks like the AB3 insurance policy for collision and med (insuring everyone in the car for up to $500) will cost us $23 the first six months, and $18 every six months following, if they are able to verify that we had a driving class in Ohio. So far the car, with everything totaled, has cost us $372.75.

Love, Dick

Dear Mom and Pop,   February 2, 1952

It took about eight hours to get back to Bethesda from home and was raining most of the way. We had no trouble and had a fairly good night's sleep.

It is now Thurs and I am three days old on my new ward which is 4-C. I am now on P.M. watch and have another corpsman that works with me. It is the Post Operative Surgery Ward and in many ways similar to my old ward (6-C). Most of the cases are appendectomy, cystectomy, or thyroidectomy. Last night I set a record in giving shots, eight in one night. We only have around 15 patients here, because they require a little more attention. A patient came in last night that [had] thought he was on the wrong train and jumped off, leaving him with a big gash in his head. They had to call out the operating crew.

During Sunday liberty, Beck, Jerry, and I took off for Annapolis and visited the Dukes. Monday night the car battery was dead, so I just walked into Bethesda and went to a movie.

Tuesday night the car was running, so I took off to see a concert by the Philadelphia Orchestra (which is supposed to be the best) at Constitution Hall. Lo and behold, as I stepped up to buy a ticket, a gentleman came up to me and said, "Want a ticket?" I said, "Sure, if you don't." I found the first couple of pieces to be very good, but then felt a little tired that night, so the soft, almost perfect music, started to work on me. Every once in a while I would wake up and listen a while before it hit me again. Oh, by the way, the ticket was worth $2.40.

Wednesday night some of the boys and I went into D.C. to see Kate McDonald and the Four Aces in a very good stage show. Guess now I will be drawing $37 rather than the usual $32 per every two weeks. Well, we have been in the service for 11 months now.

I'll bet our old classmate June Thomas figured that if she got married on our birthday, she couldn't help but be happily married (ha ha). Seems like she will need a streak of good luck somewhere. Bet it doesn't take long to name the girls we used to know that are still unmarried.

                                                    Love, Dick

Dear Ma and Pa,   February 22, 1952

Good news! I just got the Nursery (T-5) for night duty. Only when they have mothers down there, otherwise I help on T-7 which is the main Maternity Ward. Personnel called to see if I wanted to be a baby sitter. Somebody down there had such a chronic cold that he was not permitted to work around babies. I hear working up in T-5 is just as busy as any of the day shifts because the kids have to eat every four hours, day or night. Their diapers have to be changed before and after each feeding and their bottles have to be washed and autoclaved. The babies range in age from newborn to a week old. We'll also be averaging between three and five circumcisions a day. There's a special department for about six preemies.

I am now 20 years old, but don't feel any different. The nurse brought a pie for the occasion and I have half of my box of cookies and fudge on the tower. Thanks for the money, it's as good as a present.

Saw about the funniest thing the other morning I've seen since in the Navy. The other corpsman working with me was assisting the doc in starting a blood transfusion. I was in and out of the head [bathroom] while cleaning it and noticed several times that the doc was making all kinds of jabs, but wasn't having any luck hitting the vein. All of a sudden there was a big crash. When I took a peek to see what was going on, the doc was motioning to me. I headed down the hall wondering where the other corpsman went to. Well he was flat on his back under the doctor's legs and staring straight up at the ceiling. He had been holding the tube with the blood supply, so there was blood all over his whites. He had fainted dead away and was just coming to. The doc never did get the transfusion in. He said, "I can handle this. Take care of that corpsman!"

Went over to get my teeth checked at 10:00 and found out the bad news, six cavities.

Well another patient just came in, so I had better help get her in a bed.

Love, Jerry

Hi Mom and Pop,   February 27, 1952

Thanks loads for the $5 for our birthday and the candy and cookies. We sure can use the money, and the sweets were swell. We also got a box of peanuts from the Hills, a dollar a piece from Grandma and Grandpa, and cards from Ravenna Grandma, the Kent folks, Aunt Della, the Dudaks, and a few others. Thank them for us when you get a chance.

It is now Saturday night (6:00) and all is quiet up here on my ward. I have six patients and between me and Kidwell (the other corpsman) they don't keep us too busy. One of our patients died the other night from peritonitis, which is inflammation within the abdominal cavity. We have another patient on the critical list. He has a colostomy, which is a tube draining from the large intestine. He had a couple of operations and still is in rather bad condition.

We have heard tell that Shirley Temple is coming up here to have her next baby. That should be interesting.

I watched my ward doctors tie off a fellow's vein yesterday. They cut into the leg, dug down to the vein, stuck a small tube about four inches up the vein, tied the vein tightly around the tube with sutures, and then closed up the wound.

Went to a USO [United Services Organization] dance last Thursday night and found I still knew a few dance steps. Met a nice girl I will have to try and date in the future.

We finally had a flat on the car, a piece of glass as big as a fifty-cent piece. I got the tire changed and a new set of spark plugs put in. We were lucky in that the tire that got it was our bad one, instead of one of our new ones.

I received a letter from Virgil Marsh. Sounds like he's got very good duty. He's out on an island near Japan that is about 25 miles in diameter and works with 40 men and one officer. They have liberty every night and three Japanese girls clean their barracks and wash their clothes.

I am filing my income tax today, so will sign off and do so.

Love, Dick

Hi Mom and Pop,   April 9, 1952

Well I'm back on 4-C and I really like the Port and Starboard [all day on/all day off] duty schedule over the old A.M. and P.M. schedule.

They assigned me for a while on 109 which is the Communicable Diseases ward. We had lots of cases of measles, bronchial pneumonia, and pharyngitis, none of which were highly contagious, except for the measles. Those cases are kept in private rooms under isolation.

Jerry finally got in the Physical Therapy Department. Half the patients are women and the nurses (two Lieutenants) and a 3rd class Wave [that is, a female hospitalman third class] take care of them. He's given as many as eight massages in a single morning.

He does have occasional special watches. Had one with the great statesman Cordell Hull [secretary of state 1933–44] the other night. Said Hull's some man. But most of the time, instead of having watches on dying men, he just goes down to P.T. and sticks around in case something comes up.

Got a letter from Dave Green saying he was in D.C. and tried unsuccessfully to locate us. He passed all his tests and likes cadet school.

Washed and cut Jerry's hair. He also cut mine, so we look quite bare.

Tonight I'm going into Georgetown to see an old movie that I missed before, "The Snake Pit." Looks like we're both getting leaves at the end of the month. Time to muster.

Love, Dick

Dear Ma and Pa,   May 2, 1952

Dick's back on Ward 109 as galley corpsman. He's got 12 patients and things are really slow. There are some mumps, measles, and chicken pox. The other night when he got off work, he watched some of the specialists complete the remaining part of an autopsy. They had all the vital organs cut out and were starting to sew the fellow up when he got there.

Shirley Temple Black finally had her baby.

Last weekend Day, Beck and I took off for Virginia. By 2:00 P.M. we made it down to the Skyline Caverns and found them quite interesting. Then we proceeded down the Skyline Drive for about 30 miles. The drive is really something to see. It's way up in the mountains and you can see for miles off in the distance.

The other day Bobby Day plus about 24 other corpsmen took a large number of ambulatory (able to walk) patients up to the White House for a big garden party on the front lawn. Harry Truman shook hands with everybody. With Bobby being on the other shift, I don't get to see him much anymore, while Beck and Dick are on sections, so we do have the same liberty nights quite often.

There is a show opening in D.C., entitled "Skirts Ahoy" with Esther Williams who dropped in here at the Hospital this morning. She looks natural.

The latest developments on the car (new rear springs, shocks, absorbers, U boots, and rear shackles) cost a small fortune, but guess it needed them.

As far as leaves go, it doesn't look like we are going to be getting any. Guess there is becoming a shortage of corpsmen. Rather than getting schools, a lot of the corpsmen are getting orders to ship out. A new list of 25 men has been posted for the Atlantic sea coast, three of them in our class. Getting close, hey?

Glad to hear that the dogs are up to par and that the corn is in.

Love, Jerry

Dear Ma and Pa,   June 16, 1952

Now for about a month I've been on the Main Hospital Information Desk. My chief job is filing admissions and discharges and answering phone calls which come in every few minutes.

I have been switched to Sec #2 so that I can stand my weekend watches at the Information Desk. I haven't decided which is better, standing special watches, or being in here all day. Saturday morning I was the only one at the desk and it really kept me busy with two phones ringing all the time.

About 10 guys wanted to muster and three men tried to get me to log in flowers for some patients at the same time. Much fun. However, no really tough problems came up. The number of corpsmen around here is getting very thin. They put me down on the Dependent's Ward the other night with a girl about 22 who had an operation on the mitral valve of her heart. Must have been successful, because she seemed in good spirits.

The weather is really nice down here. Went golfing and hit a 60 and only lost three balls.

I haven't decided to do anything special tonight.

Love, Jerry

Hi Mom and Pop,   June 20, 1952

If the night quarters were any nicer, with air conditioning and all, we would have to start paying hotel prices.

Tomorrow will be my last night on night duty of the second week on the Dermatology Ward (skin problems, 5-B) and all the patients are ambulatory. It's an excellent ward to pull duty on. Three fourths of the patients go on liberty every night and I have no shots or medications to give what-so-ever. The bulk of my whole evening's work is the Nurse's Notes which take around one hour to complete.

One guy came in with the diagnosis of "Dermatitis Venenata," more commonly known as "Poison Ivy." What a mess! His face was swollen nearly half again its normal size. First we covered his face with corn starch (to draw on the ivy), then used a very weak solution of Sodium Hydroxin (to keep the corn starch from caking), had the lab draw a complete blood count, and gave him a shot of Cortisone. We also give him saline compresses. We had just about every doctor on the night watch up to look him over because he was such an interesting case.

Better start on my Nurse's Notes, so will have to sign off for now.

Love, Dick

Dear Ma and Pa,   June 30, 1952

I started off the other day with Chief Movahill saying, "Chappell, I'm putting you on special watch until I can get somebody up there." Well, I had that duty all day on a chap named Buzby. There was nobody to relieve me. He has his arm grafted to his leg because a growth on his leg was removed. The arm is only a means of transplanting skin from his chest to his leg.

Ever since I got to the Hospital I've heard corpsmen gripe and complain about pulling a watch on "Andy" and "Vilenzy." Well, now I've had a crack at it. Andy is an enlisted sailor who they say got plastered with liquor one night, staggered into a power house, and grabbed hold of plenty of hot wire. He weighs about a 100 pounds now, has bandages around both lower legs, his entire chest and back, and one arm. His arms and legs remind me of broom handles. Part of a thumb and two fingers are gone from his good hand.

Every time I enter his room, Andy wants me to light up a cigarette for him. After every two hours, he is ready for his narcotics shot. It takes about 15 minutes to get Andy from his bed into a chair. Those are his only two positions. If the Nurse won't let him have his shot the moment he wants it, he usually starts crying. If his bandages aren't changed often, he smells. The first day I had him, he was really in a mood where he wouldn't take his pills or let anyone touch him. Wouldn't even let me take his temperature. Since then he has been much better. He gets about 22 pills a day and when he goes to surgery to have his bandages changed, he can be heard almost all over the Hospital. One day we got him outside in the shade and some patient brought him some beer and he stayed out there all day, really satisfied.

The other chap, Vilenzy, has an adjoining room. He's in much better condition. He got rapped up in an explosion burning both arms, his sides and upper chest, and around his neck. He's lucky his face wasn't hit. The bandages around his arms and chest have to be changed everyday. I had to feed both at noon and supper. Their appetites are very good, so it's about an hour job. I was getting along really well with the boys by the end of the week. However, I hope I never have them again.

It seems like we are getting in a lot of congressmen lately. I've been escorting them around about every morning for blood work and x-rays. And on the long weekends, I've had the duty on the Information Desk as usual all day Sat. and Sun. Several premature babies died plus some chap who had hardening of the arteries, and there were some car accidents. Shirley Temple finally checked out and I never did get a good look at her.

Hope Dad had a good Father's Day. He should be getting his gift any day now. Better hit the sack now.

Love, Jerry

Hi Mom and Pop,   June 30, 1952

I have about 21 patients on my ward now but ⅔rds go on liberty, so I seldom have many here at night. Some of their skin diseases are Clomerulonephritis, Acute Acne Vulgaris Chronic, Neurodermatitis Disseminata, Dermatitis Infectiosa Eczematoides, Psoriasis Lymphogranuloma Venereal, and Basal Cell Epithelioma. Two of the fellows put ointments on their hands every night and I have to wrap all four hands and each finger separately, takes about a half hour between the two of them.

Guess whom I escorted around the Hospital the other morning? None other than Mr. Justice Hugo Black of the Supreme Court. He was here having various x-rays and tests taken.

We got the new pay raise and it gives me roughly $1.45 more every two weeks. Mathematics show that I only clear a little more than $77 a month now, but should I get 3rd class rank, I will clear over $100. That's some difference one test [a Navywide advancement examination] can make!

I got a letter off to Skip Maur and received one from both you and Freedom Grandma two days ago. Skip seems to like his job at Polson and is looking forward to college. We still haven't heard from Frank Leonard. He's probably waiting until he makes 3rd class so he can pull rank on us.

Bobby Day got back from a 15-day leave in Alabama and first thing got to see Eleanor Roosevelt who made some big speech in our Hospital auditorium. It won't be long until elections. Taft or Ike?

Sorry we did not get the leave we applied for the 27th of June, for we wanted to be home to help with the haying. Sure would have liked to get home for a few weeks to throw those hay bales around. Maybe wheat bags instead. We'll try again for around the 12th of July. The temperature has been ranging between 90 and 100 degrees for the last three days.

Love, Dick

Dear Ma and Pa,   July 5, 1952

Boy have I got news. My July 12th leave came through and I'll have a gang of days at home. The reason I got the leave is because I'm shipping out of here (the Hospital). Yeah, it's true, I'm headed back to the West coast. My orders were finally posted and they're sending me to Camp Pendleton, California to take care of the boys in the Fleet Marine Force. Since the Marines don't have any kind of medics of their own, they borrow corpsmen like us from the Navy. I'm looking at it as an okay deal because after spending liberties in the East coast cities like Baltimore and Washington, D.C., now I'll get to sample what's going on in the big cities of sunny California.

Dick is about to have kittens because his name still hasn't been posted and he has no idea where his orders are going to send him. Should find out very soon. Probably the next posting.

Got a million things to do, so you probably won't hear from me again until you see me.

Love, Jerry

Hi folks, it's me Dick—July 8. Jerry held onto his part of the letter until they posted my orders. And guess what, they aren't going to separate us again. I mean, I'm headed for Camp Pendleton right along with Jerry. We'll get leave together and head for California, probably on the same plane. Have Dad dig up some good healthy farm work for us to do, because we will see you shortly for a nice long visit.

Love, Dick

JERRY: Without doubt, it was exciting to be assigned to the Navy's biggest hospital to care for top-level officers and statesmen. We enjoyed applying our solid farm work ethics to the task of helping the sick recover. There was satisfaction in the one-on-one clinician-patient relationship.

Dick and I were always separated in our ward/tower assignments, but I do recall one patient we had in common, I think a marine captain. This client was on the Communicative Diseases Ward when Dick was on duty throughout the day shift. Toward the end of his stay on that ward, when his disease was no longer infectious, it was also recommended that he have some evening hydrotherapy in the Physical Therapy Department, where I worked the night shift. Each time I treated him in the big tub, I thought it strange that he greeted and joked with me like we were old friends. Being a very nice guy, I played along with his posture of familiarity.

About a week later he said, "Chappell, there's something I've got to tell you."

A little wary, I responded, "Oh. Like what?"

"I've got to say how much I admire you hardworking corpsmen."

I looked puzzled, "How's come?"

"Well, I've watched you work your butt off all day taking care of me and all the other brass on the disease ward . . ." I frowned to reflect confusion. ". . . then you come down here and work all night long giving hydro baths and massages. Well, it just isn't right for the Navy to work you guys so damn hard."

I finally figured out that he was one of Dick's patients, smiled, and commented, "Well thank you, Captain, we do put in our hours."

I remember another funny incident that happened to me on Tower Twelve about nine o'clock Christmas Eve. Our one patient was already sleeping, having taken a sleeping pill, and it was so quiet that Colley was back in one of the vacated rooms with the night nurse, probably just chewing the fat.

I was sitting at the front desk (which is just off the elevator) trying to stay awake (because there was nothing to do but eat candy from one of the boxes stacked on the desk). I picked up a girlie magazine that Colley had left on it just before the night nurse arrived. Since that holiday issue had a pretty

Home on fifteen-day leave, 1952, standing in front of the farmhouse

young lady on the cover that was wearing only a red and white Santa Clause hat, I picked it up and turned to throw it into the waste basket before any one could see it was there.

My mistake was that I stopped for a moment to admire the white cotton ring around the pretty young lady's red hat and I heard the elevator door slam shut. I turned around (unfortunately with the magazine still in my hand) and was stunned to see the hospital commander himself approach my desk with his hand reaching out toward me. I don't know if it was all his brass and service stripes and metals and pins or what, but I was so surprised that all I could do was hand him the girlie magazine.

Well, naturally, he frowned and brushed the magazine aside, saying, "What? At ease young man, I don't want that. I'm here to shake your hand for being on duty during the Xmas holiday and say I'm proud to command such dedicated young sailors."

By the time I gulped half a dozen times and nearly fainted as he shook my hand, he gave me the biggest box of candy (of course for everyone on Tower 12) I've ever seen and was back on the elevator. I know that was probably the dumbest thing I did in the U.S. Navy.

At some point early in our duty at the naval hospital, we learned the significance of the big bulletin board that posted outgoing assignments. As weeks passed, it became apparent that personnel only stayed in the hospital for a period of time—less than a year—and that we were temporarily in a holding pattern in a huge rotation scheme. Eventually, our new orders would ship us out; a variety of future assignments were possible. But the "posting" everyone dreaded was assignment to the Fleet Marine Force, for that meant we would end up exactly where we had worked so hard to avoid being: in the deep, muddy, cold foxhole.

A few months later, when that "worst dream" became a reality, neither Dick nor I were pleased. We even wondered if the inadvertent use of the "keeping siblings together" scheme had backfired on us. While a few corpsmen seemed excited about joining the marines, most of us felt that we were being pushed into undesired action.

DICK: We hoped for a while that we would be assigned to a hospital ship in the Korean waters. Hospital ships such as the USS *Hope* and *Consolation* had assumed a big role in the context of the Korean War. Anchored at small ports on the east coast of Korea near the thirty-eighth parallel, they had been fitted with helicopter landing platforms; patients were flown in right from the front battleline. These were emergency cases, in which speedy attention often meant the difference between life and death, or the loss or saving of a limb. In as little as five minutes, the egg-beaters could make the trip from aid station to ship, and in forty-five seconds they could unload the wounded and clear the deck. Even in choppy seas, when small boats could not be used, the helicopters carried out their mission.

Once we knew we were going to be with the Fleet Marine Force, we inquired about our designated role. We asked some of those who had been in Korea, mostly seasoned marine officers who were our patients in the hospital, and had some idea of the score. Their report of the past was not rosy. One story that I heard from someone—perhaps a doctor or marine officer who had fought in Korea only months earlier—impressed me the most. It spelled out the role doctors and corpsmen had played the first two years of the Korean War when medical teams were following troops back and forth all over the peninsula.

The story involved a naval doctor and his corpsmen assigned to the marines in their retreat from the Chosin reservoir. While studying for his M.D. he had enlisted in the U.S. Naval Reserve. In about June of 1950, following a two-year internship, he became a full-fledged doctor. When it was time for his active tour of duty in the U.S. Navy, he was transferred to the Second Battalion, Fifth Marines, out at Camp Pendleton in Oceanside, California. This new doctor, naive like us Chappell twins, was unaware the marines had no medical corps. Battle care of the wounded was all handled by the navy, and he was now a part of it.

From Pendleton, he was quickly sent to Korea, where he served with the Fifth Marines in the Inchon invasion, the recapture of Seoul, and the fight for the Chosin reservoir. His story of the marines' seventy-mile retreat from the Chosin reservoir to Hungnam reinforced our perception of the continuing nightmare. The marines had been sent up toward the Yalu River near Yudam-ni, not knowing they were going to face Chinese troops. Along with another battalion doctor and ten corpsmen, he had set up a personnel tent where they could work on the wounded. They soon heard bugles, whistles, and firing as the enemy broke through their lines. This was during thirty-degree-below-zero weather, made worse by a brutal wind chill.

Then the crucial cry "Corpsmen, corpsmen!" seemed to come from all directions. The doctor had to select and send corpsmen to meet those cries. Some came back with wounds of their own, and some never came back at all. For the rest of that night, and just about every night until they got to Hungnam, they worked on their wounded. At nighttime, the Chinese would hit them—and there the corpsmen would be, with a Coleman lamp, trying to patch someone up, set a fracture, ease pain in any way possible, while firing went on outside. The marines were often surrounded by Chinese troops; misery and death were everywhere.

It was so cold that the blood from the wounded froze on their gloves; worse still, if they took their gloves off, the blood froze their hand to the wound. If a marine had a head wound or took a bullet in the lung while out on a litter, it was nearly impossible to save him, for the blood plasma would freeze before the medical people could get it into him. The corpsmen would stuff the morphine bottles in their crotches to keep them from freezing.

In the long run the doctor was lucky, for every man who came down from Yudam-ni was either hit or had close calls. There was no such thing as a rear echelon during the march from Yudam-ni to Hungnam. The Chinese were all around them. Although no place was safe, the doctor made it safely, without so much as a sniffle.

There was some comfort for us Chappell boys in hearing that the war had become positional—and, we hoped, more stable.

Chapter Four

Fleet Marine Force Training

*W*e were flown to Camp Pendleton for a fast two-month (August and September 1952) field training period that readied us for the Fleet Marine Force. After changing from swabbie whites to marine combat uniforms, we were run through the tactics of fighting troops. We quickly made the transition from ship-based hospitalmen to battleground corpsmen. Now hospitalmen turned corpsmen, we took on the role of medical personnel who treated sick and wounded marines. The letters of this chapter describe our training for that experience.

While the farmers back in Ohio were combining crops, we Chappell twins trained to take care of marines and sailed the sea. Since we did not yet know which units we would soon join, we tried to keep abreast of what was happening in Korea. We heard that in early August, near Panmunjom, the First Marine Division lost an outpost to the Chinese. The position changed hands five times during the next two days, but the enemy eventually gained the upper hand. The marines then shifted their attack to nearby Bunker Hill (which overlooked the first outpost) and caught the enemy by surprise. Thereafter, a reinforced marine company turned back Chinese counterattacks of up to a battalion in strength. Despite the failures of these attempts, the enemy attacked twice again in August and sustained heavy casualties, in vain.

The Chinese renewed the battle of Bunker Hill in September. First they subjected the marine positions to heavy artillery and then assaulted them with a full battalion. For two hours the contest for the high ridges swung back and forth, but the marines did not give up, forcing the Chinese to back off. Over the next ten days the enemy sent a number of harassing raids against Bunker Hill, but each time the marines successfully defended their outpost. Just hearing about the fierce fighting in such battles was disheartening.

Letters

Dear Ma and Pa,   August 1, 1952

The trip out to the west coast on the large four motor United Airlines DC-6 Mainliner wasn't bad in that the planes fly smooth as silk. From the sky at night, large cities like Cleveland and Chicago sparkle just like all-colored Christmas light strings. As we came into Los Angeles between four and five their time, I noticed that the descending air pressure hurt my ears. Then it was a fair bus trip to Camp Del Mar, which is north of Camp Pendleton near Oceanside, California.

We've had it easy so far, but [we] start in the Field Medical Training School next week in Class 45 with about 50 corpsmen. The base is good sized, right next to the ocean. Besides the gang of us from Bethesda, we have some characters in our class. Three guys, who fit their descriptions, call each other "Leslie, the straight man," "Miltie, the round man," and "Bernie, the little man." The little guy is about the last one to finish anything we do and he is a comedian.

Five of us Bethesda guys had a lot of fun last weekend in Tijuana, Mexico, going to the Jai Alai games and the Bull Fight. Tijuana is strictly a tourist town and although they never have any trouble changing the American dollars, we did struggle to tell the Mexican waiters what we wanted to eat. Saturday was spent sampling Mexican food, observing the people, and seeing the city on the whole. That night we went to the fastest game in the world, spelled Jai Alai, pronounced Hi-Li. It's played with a solid granite ball, about the size of a baseball. It's thrown with terrific speed against a hard surface wall, and when it bounces off, the players catch it in a hand basket and throw it back, keeping that up until one player or team misses. You can bet on a player to win, place, or show, just like in horse racing.

Then the second sport, that we took in Sunday afternoon, which I have never seen before, was a bloody Bull Fight. The bull fighter with his red cape sees how close he can make the bull charge without hitting him. After this progresses for about 15 minutes, a man heavily armored, carrying a long pole with a sharp steel end, and mounted on a blindfolded horse (also defended heavily), jabs the bull with the sharp pole to make him more angry. As a climax, the bull fighter stabs the charging bull in a certain spot with a sword. Sometimes they have to stab it three or four times to kill it. One bull ran around for half an hour with the sword sticking all the way through him, blood spurting out the whole time.

We have gone into Oceanside to see movies on liberty, but usually just go to the base movie. The weather out here certainly isn't too hot. There's usually a cool breeze and it's easy to pick up a cold, even in our dress blue uniforms.

Love, Jerry

Hi Mom and Dad,   August 6, 1952

The Marine Corps really paid for a nice weekend for six of us Bethesda boys. They gave us $190 apiece to buy marine clothing and when we were through, the total cost was only $120, so now you know where the tax-payers money goes. We took off for L.A., looked around Hollywood, and went to the Hollywood Bowl Saturday night to see a good stage show (Cole Porter Concert). Sunday we rented a U-Drive-It car and drove up around and through Beverly Hills. I have never before seen such tremendously beautiful and gigantic homes. Every other house has either two Cadillacs or a private swimming pool. Their front lawns look more like flower gardens than lawns and each home looks like the builder tried to make it a little larger and more fancy than the guy next to him. Then we traveled up behind Beverly Hills into the mountains and saw some terrific views. The area certainly has its share of the American money.

Had steak and strawberry shortcake for dinner today. We're on the training schedule and I can see that, as in boot camp, we aren't going to have a whole lot of spare time. The first two weeks are sort of indoctrination weeks where they familiarize our class of corpsmen with the ways of the Marine Corps and give us a lot of conditioning programs to get us in shape. After another week of boot camp type military training, we will begin our medical training.

We received a worrisome letter from Frank Leonard relating that he entered the hospital with pains in the area of the heart and so forth. From the way Frank spoke in his letter, he might even get discharged and sent to a Veterans Hospital near home. If it's heart trouble, I hope that's not serious.

We will probably switch to the dress Marine suit for liberty so that we can get all our Navy clothes out of our lockers and sent home. We've gone swimming in the Pacific right here on the base. The waves are big and the sand soft, but the water is cold.

Dick and Jerry in marine dress wools, with "Ike" jackets

It was quite a surprise yesterday when six guys we knew well in Bethesda came down on the next F.M.F. draft, including Bobby Day. All the drafts have been going either to here or Camp Lejeune [North Carolina]. Don Beck got an air craft carrier.

My address will be R. G. Chappell, HN [Hospital Corpsman] 571-80-61, FLD. Med. Trng. BN. Class 45, T and R Comd. CJHP, Camp Del Mar, Oceanside, California. Jerry's will be the same. Glad to hear that your weather is permitting some combining.

Love, Dick

Hi Mom and Dad,   August 26, 1952

When Marine sergeants teach us Marine tactics, they don't miss a thing. We've learned much about the Marine Corps and all the subdivisions that compose it, how they operate in combat such as offensive and defensive tactics, the different types of weapons and most accurate use of each and many other things in general.

We are ready for whatever type of work we get into with the Marine operations and combat tactics. We can now tear down, clean, put together and fire the U.S. Rifle Cal. .30 M-1, the U.S. Carbine Cal. .30 M-2, and the U.S. Pistol Cal. .45. They taught us more about guns in two days than the Navy taught us in two weeks at Boot Camp. With our issue of clothing, they also gave us a complete pack, and along with our military training we have had several long hikes in which we carried the packs. They get heavy after a hike of eight or nine miles.

At the end of our two weeks of military training we went out into the hills of Camp Pendleton and spent the night in the wide open in sleeping bags. The whole two day program was called a bushwhack and brought back memories of Boy Scout camping days. We used blanks in our guns and played war with the Seabees [navy construction battalion personnel]. We had fun and I think it was a tie. Since they worked us hard, I'm getting back in shape and my appetite is amazing compared to what it used to be.

Along with our conditioning program, every other day we had to run over an obstacle course that consists of rope climbing, log walking, board leaping, rope swinging, etc. About ⅓ of the fellows never made it over the complete course. Jerry and I both made it the first time we tried and each time we went over it, it got a little easier.

Now to bring you up to date on the classwork part of our training. We are into eight hour days reviewing medical data on shock, hemorrhage, wounds, applying bandages, etc., just like we did in the Hospital Corps Training School. Bobby Day is in Class 46 and will start the schedule next week.

Now about our liberties, the four of us, Grame, Day, Jerry and myself all took off for Mexico again and took in several floor shows and the Hi-Li games for a swell time. Five of us also rented a car for 28 hours and followed along the oceanside drive up through Laguna, Long Beach, and into L.A. After a night in a hotel, we continued on to Pasadena, California, and circled south to arrive back in Oceanside about 6:00, covering some 288 miles.

The pictures I'm sending home show both of us, Pankus with rifle and helmet (a Bethesda boy), Kirkland who was one of my classmates at Bainbridge and has been with us all the way, and that's Jerry hanging from a rope on part of the obstacle course.

Love, Dick

Dear Ma and Pa,   September 5, 1952

Our taste of military training is over. We got into the hills and it was fun playing war with the Seabees using blanks in our M-1s. We got sick of cleaning our M-1s, but now that is over and we have turned them in. Our whole

Jerry in physical-endurance training on the Camp Pendleton obstacle course

class moved out to Tent Camp 2, attached to the Headquarters and Service Company. Our medical training is the same old stuff (classes, studying, and tests). Most of our instructors are chiefs and some of them are really good. We've been going back in the hills for classes on sanitation to learn the best ways to sterilize eating gear, build latrines, etc. We slept out in large hospital tents which we learned to put up.

Some of the young Marine 2nd Lieutenants that are just out of officer training are really strict. When they give a command, they expect us corpsmen to jump. This morning we had two hours of drill marching and may get some more this afternoon. If our outfit isn't snappy enough to suit them, they have threatened to give us either weekend restriction from liberty or the choice of climbing up a mile-and-a-half mountain with full pack on. They have some mountains right around our camp that really go up. A six foot Mormon from Utah, named Albertson, and I climbed one yesterday. You can see for miles.

Remember you sent that article about the evacuation of the wounded in Korea. Well those evacuation teams are a small part of the large network

Dick learning field
maneuvers and the use
of Marine Corps
weapons

of evacuation stations. It takes many corpsmen to evacuate and care for the
wounded as they are transferred from the front, back to battalion aid stations,
back to Regimental Aid Stations, back to hospital-like collecting and clearing
stations, and back to a hospital ship or Korean or Japanese hospitals, and then
back to a hospital in the states. It is quite an organization and amazing the
rapid speed at which they can get a casualty out. By the looks of the training
we have been getting, there is a possibility that we may become part of that
network.

Love, Jerry

Hi Mom and Pop,   September 11, 1952
    Last weekend was one of our best and we really had a wonderful time. Our
liberty started Friday evening, and Dick Holt, Kirkland, and the two of us
took off for L.A. by Greyhound bus. We were lucky enough to get tickets (excellent seats, second row, dead center, about 10 feet from the actors) for the
last matinee of "South Pacific" for Saturday afternoon. Janet Blair played the
lead part well both as an actor and a singer. The music by Rogers and Ham-
merstein was very good. Loved all the nurses and Seabees. In the evening
we got tickets to "The Moon is Blue," which was also an excellent play with

Dick and Coy Brewer playing with a football during time off for recreation

Dina Lynn, David Niven, and Scott Brady. We spent lots of money, because it was probably our last weekend in the states for a few months.

I've included 10 pictures of us including some of our recreation times.

Love, Dick

Dear Ma and Pa,   September 12, 1952

Here's the scoop. We are taking off about the 14th on a transport ship for a two-week cruise to Japan. We sail up toward "Frisco" and pick up the rest of the fleet. This is our chance to see if we like sea duty and if we get sick or not. Virgil's letters claim that Japan is quite the place to see, so in a way we are looking forward to it. Who knows maybe we can send you some good souvenirs. All the troops that we will be traveling with are going to end up in Korea.

We will spend the remaining time that we are here in the states assembling our gear and packing it away. They told us before that tonight would be our last liberty before we board the ship, but rumors are that they may break-down and give us till Sunday morning.

So, my old high school flame, Jane Wiedeman, is now married to a farmer. Good for her! Most of our class of 50 are either married or in the service. Where is their farm? Has it started to cool down back home, or are you in "Indian Summer?"

Love, Jerry

Dear Mom and Dad,   September 16, 1952

Well at last we have reached our living quarters on our ship, the USNS *Marine Serpent*. Our mailing address for the next couple of weeks will be: Richard G. Chappell, HN, 571-80-62, [and] Gerald E. Chappell, HN, 571-80-61 USN, 24th Company, 3rd Replacement (Ground), c/o Fleet Post Office, San Francisco, California.

There are around 2500 men on the ship and everything is crowded. They are fairly good sized compartments with gobs and gobs of racks four layers high. I have a top one, and if I turn over slowly, I can miss the ceiling. However, they are comfortable and I won't have to worry about anybody getting sea sick and vomiting on me. Good logic, hey! Without leaving my rack, I can touch about 10 guys, so you can see it's close quarters. We have to keep whatever gear we have in the bunks with us. I'm next to a light and a fresh air vent, so I'm well set.

We are now rolling and tossing in the waves of the wide Pacific Ocean. The *Serpent* is not a large ship in comparison to the average naval vessel. Its main purpose is to transport troops and not comfort. The old *Serpent* is supposed to shove off about 1600 tonight. They say you never get the full appreciation of home and the U.S. until you have had a cruise to another country, so now is our chance. If you have any trouble reading this, it's because I'm writing on the ceiling rather than the floor. I guess the proper names are overhead and deck.

Love, Dick

Dear Ma and Pa,   September 20, 1952

I have now regulated myself to sea-going life, and I don't think too much of it. Our quarters are right at the front and just below the main deck. We only climb one flight of stairs to get on deck, which is good because this old girl gets to rolling like mad and three or four stairs are an effort.

The chow is good most of the time, except we have no milk. It's coffee for every meal. Everybody is hungry because there is very little to do but think about the next meal.

The first couple of days out were peaceful, so hardly anybody got sick. About the 3rd day those who were going to get sick did so. It's comical to watch them run for the rail to vomit or better yet [in] the G.I. Can. After the 3rd day we hit not really bad but not good weather, and it's been that way ever since. There is no fog or rain, but there is a strong wind which keeps the waves rolling and the ship rocking up and down. Most of the time it is difficult to stand up without holding onto something. Sometimes, where I sleep, the ship lifts and drops two or three feet back and forth with me rolling from one side on my rack to the other each time. Some fun, hey! Surprising though, I sleep good, usually hitting the rack between nine and 10 and rising at 0600.

About the 5th day out I had some scrambled eggs for breakfast that didn't set right, so I ended up losing my chow before the morning was over. Ever since then as long as I get three warm meals a day, I feel very good.

I'd better sign off and do my detail.

Love, Jerry

Hi Mom and Dad,   September 24, 1952

This is our 9th day at sea and so far I haven't got sea sick. It is a wonder though because the sea has been tossing this ship around, making half the guys sick at one time or another. At night, when sleeping, we roll from one side of the bunk to the other and during chow our trays slide back and forth. This might be the peaceful Pacific, but I haven't seen anything peaceful about it yet. Kirkland got sick the second day and has been sick most of the time since.

We have half an hour of cleaning up in the mornings and the rest of the time we spend playing cards and reading novels.

The ship puts out a small pamphlet newspaper which keeps us up to date on the news. We have a small recreation room, which seats about 200, where our movies are run.

We passed the international date line, so today is Thursday Sept. 25 instead of Wednesday Sept. 24. The imaginary line, accepted by all countries is a line running more-or-less North and South. Occasionally, its path is erratic in order to bypass islands or land masses. A dateline running through an island could be fertile nervous-breakdown territory for confused inhabitants. For instance, the line deviates from the 180th Meridian around the Aleutian Islands, so that all the islands have the same time as the United States. Further north it swerves again to prevent time-slicing an eastern mass of Russian territory. In the South Pacific, the line repeatedly deviates to pass land masses. As of last night, we are now on Asiatic time. But cheer up, coming back we'll pick up the day we lost. According to tradition, certificates of crossing the 180th Meridian will be passed to all hands. Monday afternoon they had to stop the ship while a doctor performed an appendectomy, which, with the tossing of the ship, was no easy operation. The results were a success.

This morning while we were standing in chow line a big wave came up on the ship and soaked us completely. We saw a ship pass this morning and there were two whales spotted yesterday. We've also seen a lot of jellyfish which light up the water at night.

We are getting a lot of back letter writing done, including two to you, Kenny Kline, Virgil Marsh, Frank Leonard, Ronnie Newcome, Don Beck, and a few others. Saturday night our Company got to play Bingo, but we were not lucky enough to win anything.

What did you think of the Rocky Marciano–Joe Walcott fight? The best man (Marciano) won in my opinion.

Love, Dick

Dear Ma and Pa,   September 30, 1952

Finally, after about 12 days at sea, the large waves have ceased and the ocean is reasonably calm. Now that we are used to the continual motion of the ship, it doesn't bother us anymore. Most of the fellows that were seasick have recovered. The last few days the weather changed from cold to warm and the ocean is calmer and the days sunny.

We will arrive in Kobe, Japan, Wednesday morning. In Kobe we all get our orders, so we may stay there or move on to Korea. I am sending a few things home that I didn't want to take a chance on losing such as my drivers license and a certificate that the ship created showing we have crossed the 180th meridian.

Except for the half hour morning details and a couple of musters, we have had things pretty much to ourselves. Everybody on ship is thinking about what kind of meal they are going to buy when they get to Kobe. We have some small books on Japanese language, so I have been trying to pick up a few phrases. We have to change some of our American money into scrip and then Japanese money.

How is the car holding up? Has it given you any trouble since the battery went dead? We will write to you all about Japan, if we get the liberty we are hoping for. Inspection time.

Love, Jerry

Reflections

JERRY: There was nothing boring about learning the basics of what it was like to be a marine infantryman. They ran us through drills with all kinds of weaponry (hand grenades, the M-1, and especially the revolver and carbine that we would carry in the war zone), got us in shape on the obstacle course, and focused our medical skills on war injuries.

I remember how much we wanted to be ready for anything and everything. So, during our free time in the evenings, we engaged in additional conditioning by running up and down a nearby mountainside. Dick and I, and our friend Bruce Albertson, also spent extra time practicing such rescue tactics as throwing a casualty over our shoulder, then carrying the wounded to a safe spot. That practice went pretty well until it was time to haul Albertson off the battlefield, for the guy weighed more than two hundred pounds (of solid muscle).

There was one training drill in which we practiced jumping into the waist-deep water off a small landing craft. Then we had to dash through the water with a carbine held high, our heavy backpacks feeling as if they could push us nose-down any minute. The drill ended with us charging (slipping) up a sandy beach and digging in before enemy bullets knocked off our helmets. I knew it was only a drill (no real rounds were fired at us), but it was surprising how fast my body could be sapped of energy and how my legs felt like they were made of rubber. Obviously, just training for the dangers of action in a war zone made me feel my life could be cut short really soon.

Although none of us corpsmen talked much about it (while training or on liberty), we all knew that once overseas we might never see the United States of America again. In our last weeks, Dick and I headed for Tijuana, Mexico, with several other fellow trainees, just to have as much fun as possible before shipping out. I guess we thought there was safety in numbers, in that with the group we wouldn't drink too much or get in trouble with wild Mexican women. I remember going into a tavern to have some drinks and watch gals striptease. After we had watched and drunk for a while, we must have made a hit with the girls, for the next thing we knew, each one of us had one sitting on our lap teasing us one way or another. Mine wasn't quite Miss Mexico, but she sure could get a guy worked up. Anyhow, by the time she had swiped my glasses and slipped them into her panties to get them all steamed up, I signaled to the rest of the guys (who were in similar trouble) that we had better get the hell out of there while we still had our pants on. When we got back to base, I wondered just how smart we had been. Maybe we should have stayed for at least one more beer.

DICK: Even the ship's newspaper kept us abreast of the war happenings in Korea, and the news usually was not good. That same paper that congratulated us on crossing the 180th meridian line (September 25) gave us the following update:

COMMIES LOSE HILL, 4 AIRCRAFT

Tokyo—Counter attacking allied troops recaptured a strategic peak Monday a few hours after a North Korean battalion had seized the hill in the heaviest Communist assault in three months on the Eastern front. The United Nations forces clawed their way back to the crest of the height near another "Luke the Gook's Castle" in three tank backed surges between dawn and four P.M. The hill is northeast of "The Punchbowl," a circular valley 15 miles north of Inje, a hamlet just inside North Korea on the Eastern front. US Sabre-Jets damaged four MIGs in two air battles over northwest Korea. The September toll of MIGs rose to 102, fifty destroyed, four probably destroyed, and 48 damaged. That tied the record monthly score for the entire war. The fighting on the western front died down. US 2nd Division troops were digging in on top of "Old Baldy."

Amongst our corpsmen's group on the USNS *Marine Serpent,* there was much talk of the progress of the Korean War and what awaited us if we were assigned to a fighting unit in the heart of the war. We knew the enemy were continuously building up their artillery. The word was that in one day in September 1952, more than 45,000 rounds had fallen on the Eighth Army front.

We knew also that the reality of our worst dream was on the horizon. We would be assigned to some fighting marine unit in the heart of the Korean War. We would end up on a main line of resistance in the midst of deep-dug bunkers, trenches, barbed-wire defenses, and extensive outposts where most of the action took place. Since the battle and nonbattle casualties had been heavy, we expected they would continue to be so. If it were not for battlefield medical innovations—mobile army surgical hospitals (MASH units), air evacuation, rest and relaxation ("R and R") in Japan—both categories of casualties (war and nonwar) would be even heavier. The possession of dominating outpost heights, for observation and use of artillery and mortars, was important, so the fights along the outpost line had been, and would be, bloody and persistent. In July and August there had been long periods of lull because of the heavy rains, but whenever weather allowed the enemy had made fierce efforts to capture and cling to the UN outpost positions. In turn, we did not like hearing that the enemy periodically tried to penetrate our positions on the main line of resistance. They always relied on their tactic of sending a hoard of troops, without regard to losses.

Chapter Five

The Main Line
of Resistance

The letters of this chapter share our perceptions on life on the main line of resistance, known as the MLR—life in bunkers, on outposts, and on patrols in search of the enemy. The map traces important phases of the 1952 operations and locates key hills and ridges on the western and central fronts of the MLR, where Eighth Army action was concentrated. The area was called the most dangerous strip of ground on earth.

The MLR was a deep trench, from five to seven feet in depth, running along the ridgeline of the hills. Theoretically, the MLR was a continuous trench avenue that ran from coast to coast, cutting the peninsula of Korea in half.

We were lucky to be on the front line during a two-month period when, except for a few incidents, there was a relative lull for the Fifth Marine Regiment. However, we learned through "scuttlebutt" that passed from bunker to bunker that other points on the MLR were not so lucky. On the western hills near the Chorwon Valley, seven Chinese regiments had spent three weeks trying to take White Horse Hill from the Republic of Korea Ninth Division. The ROKs, as we called them, had held out at the cost of 3,500 casualties, inflicting close to ten thousand Chinese casualties. As a counteraction, General Van Fleet launched in October an attack (called Operation Showdown) a little farther east, near the village of Kumhwa. The Chinese decided they wanted to keep those hills, so the battle continued for six weeks, ending after about ten thousand UN casualties and about twenty thousand Communist.

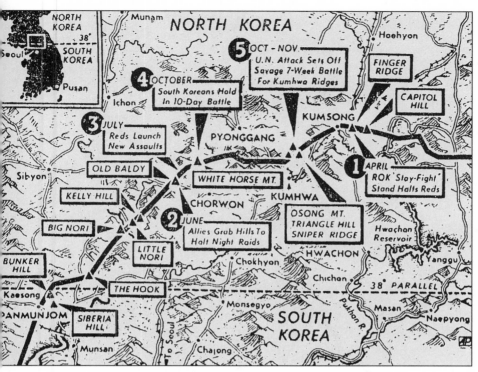

The Eighth Army review (in the *Stars and Stripes*) of the 1952 Korean battle line identified the UN forces below the line and the North Korean Communist forces above it.

The drawing of the Western Korean First Marine Division Front shows that while units of the Korean Marine Corps defended the left regimental sector, the First, Fifth, and Seventh Marine Regiments alternated turns in running the center and right sectors along with the outposts immediately in front of those. One regiment of the First Marine Division was always in reserve.

Our Fifth Marines returned to the MLR on October 12–13, 1952 (about the time we joined them) and remained in combat until November 25, 1952. Our Second Battalion was on Line "Jamestown," occupying the right sector of the regiment's area (Fox ["F"] Company on the left side, Dog ["D"] Company in the center, and Easy ["E"] Company on the right); we also manned outposts "Ava," "Corrine," "Dagmar," "Esther," and "Ginger." On November 16, Easy Company moved left of Fox Company to man outposts "Bunker" and "Hedy" as well. Other battalions of the Fifth Marines held a set of forward outposts known as the "Nevada cities" ("Vegas," "Carson," and "Reno"),

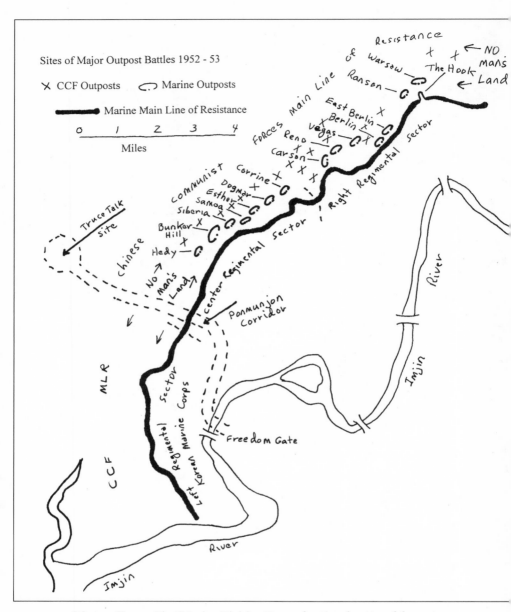

Sites of Major Outpost Battles 1952 - 53

X CCF Outposts   ◠ Marine Outposts

━━━● Marine Main Line of Resistance

0   1   2   3   4

Miles

Resistance
of Warsaw
The Hook
NO MANS Land

Forces Main Line
Ranson
East Berlin
Berlin
Reno
Vegas
Carson
Corrine
Dogmar
Esther
Samoa
Siberia
Bunker Hill
Hedy

Communist
Chinese
No Mans Land

Truce Talk Site

Right Regimental Sector

Center Regimental Sector

Ponmunjon Corridor

MLR

Sector

Left Regimental

Korean Marine Corps

CCF

Freedom Gate

River

Imjin

River

Imjin

Western Korean First Marine Division Front, showing the sites of the major
outpost battles of 1952–53

as well as "Berlin" and "East Berlin." In addition to daily sniper fire, during that time the Second Battalion's sector and outposts received from twenty to 230 rounds daily, an average of about 135, of artillery, mortar, and rocket fire.

When we were placed in reserve after November 25, we had a chance to move around, meet guys from other companies, and share stories about what we had experienced or heard. We learned that late in October, while our combat action had been mostly limited to small-unit clashes (outpost attacks, raids, and patrols), marine sectors on both sides of us had been hit hard. Units of the Seventh Marine Regiment (on our eastern flank, or right side) had lost over seventy men (nearly four hundred wounded and forty missing) fighting back and forth against Chinese communist forces of battalion strength for outposts "Ransom" and "Warsaw" and a forward-looping section of the MLR call "the Hook." After being bombarded by twenty-five hundred rounds of Chinese artillery and mortar fire, Korean marines on our western flank, or left side, had lost fifty men (over eighty wounded and about twenty missing) repelling the assaults of eight companies against four of their outposts.

The marines took good care of us corpsmen. Our bunkers were generally among the more secure ones. We usually found our quarters, and even our positions on outposts and patrols, right in the heart of the C.P. (command post), with the lieutenant and the radioman.

Letters

Dear Mom and Dad,   October 22, 1952

Happy Birthday Dad! Eat a piece of that birthday cake for me. Our chance of getting a gift for you, or even to write, has been slim the last month.

After nine days on the front line, all is well. As of yet, I haven't received any mail from you, but did get a letter from Jerry which included your letter.

The first night we arrived here on the front line was the worst. Under the cover of pitch darkness, they trucked us up to the nearby staging area with full packs, all our gear, and guns in hand. It was scary with mortar rounds exploding and lighting up the night at distant points in all directions. It was one of the coldest nights I can remember as we slept in tents that had little or no heat and hard cots.

The Chief in Charge recommended that, being twins, we split up. Well, of course we split up, Jerry going to Easy Company, and me to Fox Company. I don't think I slept at all that night, and it sure wasn't much of a "Welcome to the front lines of Korea."

I certainly get plenty to eat out here. We have the handiest little stoves that really do the trick of heating or cooking chow. The rear supply area sends up lots of exchange supplies to the front lines free of charge, so we usually get loads of candy bars and the guys that smoke never have to worry about cigarettes.

We use candles in the evening to light up our bunkers. Three of us, the radio man, myself, and a company runner have a whole bunker to ourselves with plenty of room to store our gear. There was even a couple of sexy pin up pictures left for us by the guys we relieved. Just like home (ha ha).

I am pleased with the fellows that compose my platoon. Some of the old salts say that we have it nice compared to the last time Fox Company was on the MLR (Main Line of Resistance). That suits me just fine and I hope it remains that way.

My new mailing address is: Richard G. Chappell, HN, 571-80-61, F 2/5 1st Marine Division, c/o F.P.O., San Francisco, Calif.

Love, Dick

Dear Ma and Pa,   October 31, 1952

You ought to see me now. I'm somewhere between nine and 10 thousand miles from home out in an outpost bunker for a few days. Instead of my swanky little bunker on the MLR (Main Line of Resistance), I am now sleeping in one that's maybe a hundred yards out into the no man's land that I can't even stand up in. I moved out here after a big rain and at first it was all mud. I'm glad I wasn't here when the rain was coming down, because all the bunkers leak like sieves.

A Lieutenant, a 1st sergeant, and I sleep side by side and all I have to do is stand the phone watch ⅓ of the night and most of the day. This whole area is mostly hills with bunker lines running along the MLR in zig zag patterns. Out here there's a short trench line connecting about six Marine bunkers. The job of the outpost guys is to alert the troops on the MLR in the case of any Gook jump-off attacks. I don't have to leave my bunker as long as everybody keeps their heads down. Fortunately, the Gooks don't like the rain and mud any more than we do and so it's been quiet out here. Don't worry, we'll get along fine with all our Boy Scout and Marine Corps training.

Lieutenant Cullom is a big boy who claims he played football with the New York Giants against the Cleveland Browns not very long ago.

I just finished heating up a can of ground meat and spaghetti for chow. Not bad, but I'm getting tired of being my own cook. There's a lot of difference between my cooking and your cooking. If you do send us a can of cider, its bite will be just about right when it gets here (ha ha). Another thing to send to me would be some of the sexy books you see in drug stores, because the boys really go for that kind of reading stuff.

I got your letter in seven days and will forward it on to Dick. So you had a visit from Kenny Kline, hey. His leave must have been almost a month. Those guys in the Air Force have it made. It's good to hear that you have a box of goodies on the way. Before I came out here, Mac (Dave MacGowan), my fellow corpsman, got a 5-pound fruit cake (took a month to arrive) and it was gone by night time.

My little MLR hospital bunker is like a warm-up bunker. Just about everyone in the platoon drops in at least once a day for a piece of toast and butter. One day we used the stove to toast four loaves. I had about half a loaf myself with jam. Number 1.

Our new platoon Lieutenant is fresh out of Officer Candidate School. The hard chargers in the platoon don't quite know what to think of him yet. He's a little on the feminine side, so he is referred to as "her," "she," or "Mrs."

Love, Jerry

Hi Mom and Dad, November 1, 1952

We have now been up on the front line for 19 days. I believe our area is a little more active than Jerry's.

Save that article on "Treat Them Up Front." I don't know whom the article was written about, but I'm sure they can't out do us Naval-Marine medics. So far I have treated 10 casualties and all are doing okay now.

You asked about how we treat shock when a Marine is injured. While in school we received a good basic knowledge on wound treating and shock, but the best teacher is first hand experience. When we first reach our casualty (and acceptable conditions prevail), we give them a shot of Morphine ($\frac{1}{2}$ grain), which is an opium derivative that has a powerful drug action that decreases the amount of pain. Naturally, we have to stop any bleeding and prevent infection or further injury by applying battle dressings.

Verbal psychiatry can aid in the prevention of shock. Or, if the casualty has already gone into a state of shock, we inject a fluid into the vein that combats it physically. It's all in a day's work. Usually it's less than an hour, and seldom more than two, until the patient has been seen by a doctor and is on his way to a rear area hospital or hospital ship. The helicopter plays a large part in our evacuation program.

I would guess that at least $\frac{1}{3}$ of our casualties are flown out to a hospital ship right from in back of the front lines. Generally a fellow has to be shot up seriously, or has broken bones, before a copter is sent for. The reason the

Marines are such good fighting men is because they know they have the best medical support behind them.

I hear from Jerry regularly and things are going well over in his area also. Glad to hear the good news about Frank Leonard. That will be swell, if he can go back to college. I also got a letter from Don Beck who is working long hours on the naval [aircraft] carrier.

I am sending a check home for you to stash in a bank for me. I'm also sending 2000 won of Korean money home. Since 6000 won make one American dollar, you'll get about 33 cents. Most Koreans run around with a big stack of won that make them look like millionaires, but actually it's only a small amount. It takes 30 of the larger bills to make $5 of our money.

After hours of thought, I have finally decided what you can send me for Xmas. That's a handy-to-carry, not too large, medical book with illustrations and definitions, if possible. As of yet, I don't know what or when we can buy anything for you folks.

Love, Dick

Dear Ma and Pa,   November 8, 1952

Time is passing quickly and I've only had 12 casualties at this point. I was glad to hear we're going to stay in this position until about the 15th. The Gooks have me baffled in that it seems they have taken all their men over to distant Triangle Hill.

We get to see a lot of jets drop Jelly [napalm] Bombs and strafe the Gooks on their MLR two or three times a day. Our white-phosphorus bombs and rockets make some fireworks at night time.

Another sergeant moved in with us when Mac went out to the Outpost for about five days. Mac treated the first casualty out there from our 3rd platoon. He's from Akron and has been in the service for about five years and has shipped over for another three. He was stationed at Bethesda Hospital for three years and worked on almost every ward there. He then volunteered for the Fleet Marine Force and was with the 3rd Division for about 15 months. He will be replaced with another corpsman before too long and I will be the old timer.

Yes, we are in the First Marine Division, which is divided up into three Regiments. The 7th and 5th (us) Regiments are up on the MLR now. It's the 7th Regiment that is getting all the fighting and have been hit hard. We of the 5th are positioned to their right flank and seem to be left alone. Once a week we get the Korean "Stars and Stripes" Newspaper.

This morning it snowed, but was gone by the time I got up at 10 o'clock. Our caps have ear protection and we have good gloves for the cold weather.

Bunker and trench along the MLR (main line of resistance)

We used wood from ammo boxes and cardboard from C-ration boxes to make the floor in our bunker. Another gang of rats moved into our bunker, so last night I put out eight crackers with poison on them. Since they took six of them, we should have some results.

Today we are having an inspection of our positions by some big shot, so everybody had to shave, take off their dirty dungarees, and put on their less dirty dungarees. A barber came up from the rear to give everybody haircuts.

I just put out the stove, for the Gooks were zeroing in on the smoke. They missed the bunker.

We just had payday and I now have $170 on the books. I haven't heard yet, but there is a slight chance I passed the 3rd class [petty officer] test (HM3) [hospital corpsman third class] and have money there from the higher rank. I haven't spent more than a dollar since I've been in Korea.

Love, Jerry

Dear Ma and Pa,   November 9, 1952

Our boys still don't think too much of our new Lt., as he seems to think we are all on a big camping expedition.

We have heard that Ike has been elected President. Must be Adlai's [Stevenson] speeches weren't hot enough. Rumor is that he's coming over to visit us.

The Lt's name from the outpost that played football was Cullom. He played mostly offensive backfield and got clobbered one game 57 to zero. I just returned from church. We are waiting for the 26th draft of corpsmen to come in to see if it includes our friend Bobby Day. We know some of them are coming to our battalion.

We've had nearly a month of front line duty. The 1st platoon had a few more casualties, but so far my old 3rd is riding easy. I hear from Dick about every week, and he says things are quiet over there also. However, tomorrow is the Marine Corps birthday and I'm anxious to see if the Gooks make all the noise they are supposed to.

I haven't been down to the showers or changie-changie for a couple of weeks now and am getting scroungy. I had some boil trouble lately, on my neck, that is slowly going away.

We get quite a bit of candy in with our PX [post exchange, i.e., ship's service store] rations and I've been swapping my allotment of cigarettes for hot chocolate. I use a few of the cartons to fill rat holes. Sounds like Dad is getting caught up in the farm work. I've got to sign off for now.

Love, Jerry

Hi Mom and Dad, November 12, 1952

A month of front line duty and all is well. Mail has been coming in good with the exception of one thing, no news on the HM3 test results.

No, we never wash clothes up here on the line. Every chance we get, which is about every 12 days, we drop back into a rear area and get a shower plus a complete change of clothes. Late the day before yesterday (the Marine Corps Birthday) we started getting hot meals brought up in food thermals that keep it warm. We never had it before, because it was the custom to have one central eating place. And, well, if a round happened to hit that one spot, then there would be a lot of casualties. That very thing happened a week ago in Dog Company, killing three men and wounding about 15 others. Must have kept the corpsmen jumping! By using thermals, the chow is split up and delivered to three sections instead of one place. We even had cake and ice cream.

Love, Dick

Dear Ma and Pa, November 12, 1952

We have had some action around here lately. Three nights ago my platoon pulled a raid on a hill. There were 80 of us with only myself and another corpsman. Luckily we ran into some Gook [barbed] wire right at the base of

Dick (right front) with a squad from Second Platoon, Fox Company, Second Battalion, Fifth Marine Regiment, First Marine Division

the hill, which was 30 foot wide and over our heads. Some of our guys tried setting it off with demolition charges and everything, but it just bounced. In the meantime, we were all standing in water over our knees. Fortunately, there were no casualties for the old 3rd platoon due to the wire holding us back.

On the night of the 11th, the unlucky 1st platoon pulled a raid on another hill. They got hit badly, with our Commanding Officer getting killed. My bunker was used for the smaller casualties with two other bunkers for the worst cases. I patched up eight guys myself. None of them too bad. We had a doctor up here all night. Mac performed an arm amputation all by himself. There was a newspaper man on the raid, so you might possibly hear something about it.

It's been cool and rainy lately. Things are back to normal today.

Love, Jerry

Hi Mom and Dad,   November 15, 1952

Today marked the end of our 33 days on the line and all is well. We have had very few casualties lately, with the exception of two today and two yesterday. None of them were serious, with just arm and leg wounds. So far, out

The Fox Company first-aid bunker on the front line

of the 13 men I have treated, only three were suffering so badly that I had to give them morphine.

Here's the way corpsmen are placed in a company. Each company has three platoons with two corpsmen per platoon and one corpsman acting as the man in charge of the other six. Which adds up to seven per company.

My co-worker (Fine) and I have around 65 men attached to our platoon. The seven corpsmen are split up between about 240 men per company

The company is commanded by a Marine Captain, and each platoon by a 2nd Lieutenant. We had a "number 1" (that's the expression used over here for being the best) 2nd Lt. up til two days ago when he shipped out for Japan duty. A new one took over yesterday and everybody is wondering how he will turn out under a little combat action.

Next in command in a platoon (under the 2nd Lt.) is the Platoon Sergeant (ours is a Sergeant Louder), who is a number 1 man.

Each platoon has three squads of 12 men, plus three squad leaders. Also, there is a machine gun section of three or four guns and a mortar section.

Each platoon of a Marine company has *tak-a-son* (that's Korean for a large amount) of fire power with all kinds of automatic weapons. Old "Luke the Gook" thinks twice before he tangles with my 2nd Platoon, Fox Company.

We really have a happy little C.P. Group in our 2 bunkers which are right together. The seven of us include the Lt., Sergeant Louder, us two corpsmen, the right guide (supply man for the platoon), and two radio men.

Every night when we are not engaged in some activity, we make cocoa and hold a regular gab session. However, most nights something usually breaks it up.

We all got our feet fitted today for thermal boots which we should get in a week or so. Also, got inner linings for our field jackets and winter breaker pants.

Every day and night they send KSC [Korean Service Corps. A republic of Korea quasi-military organization of civilians for labor in support of UN Forces] workers up to help dig trenches and fill sand bunkers. Some of them are really characters and they always leave the oldest *papa-san* (oldest man) at the C.P. to clean up and do odd jobs.

I have to go, so will sign off for now.

Love, Dick

Dear Ma and Pa, November 18, 1952

A lot has happened in the last few days. Saturday night we moved out of our old position and were hauled by trucks back to Battalion Reserve. Sunday morning I got up in time for church services, followed that with a hot meal, then got a changie-changie and a hot shower (first one in three weeks). I sure needed one.

I got my gear packed up and took off to Item [that is, "I"] Company to see old Grame and Franklin. Both were looking good and have been in Reserve since we got here. I ate chow with Holt. He's with the Weapons Company and did get to see some action on the MLR. About dark we pulled out to our new position by Fox Company. Two squads and I slept in a big hospital bunker they are building a distance behind the lines. We have added three new corpsmen to our company (one from Class #46), so Mac will get relieved in six days. About 2:30 I took off for Fox Company. Saw Dick and ate chow with him. He's looking good and playing it cool.

My Company (Easy) now has a platoon-size area on the MLR, and two outposts, to man. The 1st platoon is on the line and my platoon is out on the Bunker Hill outpost. At one time this was the hot spot on the MLR, but times change and now it is fairly quiet. I think we will be out here about six days. I sleep with two other guys in a bunker. We've gotten some new winter gear.

It was good to hear that my money allotment came home. I'll be making $155 now with combat pay. Be sure to take out all expenses for shipping the gear and take out a nice sum for each of you to buy a X-mas gift of some kind.

Love, Jerry

Dear Ma and Pa,   November 23, 1952

I finished three days and nights out on the outpost (my platoon is still out there) with only one casualty. I was glad everyone mostly stayed in their bunkers. Now I'm back on the MLR (temporarily with the 1st Platoon) safe and sound. However, just as we were coming off, two mortar rounds dropped right in the middle of five men. None of them were hurt bad, and with four of us corpsmen, we patched them up in a hurry.

I got up this morning, shaved off six days of beard, and went down to the first aid bunker. To my surprise your first box was waiting with figs, raisons, shoestrings, candles (still worth their weight in gold over here), nuts and a fruit cake. Ate the fruit cake in the bunker of the first squad of the 3rd Platoon. Then took the rest up to the 1st Platoon.

Our Lt received 22 packages while he was out on the outpost for three days. He comes from a rich family and they really send him the stuff.

We did get our Mickey Mouse boots and cold weather parkas while we were out there. They are warm and make us look like Eskimoes. Right now I'm glad that my co-working corpsman, Mac (Dave), is being relieved by a corpsman with a lot of experience.

Love, Jerry

Hi Mom and Dad,   November 28, 1952

We had a big Thanksgiving with turkey and all the trimmings. It was really a number one meal.

With the exception of a Korean worker that got burned on the hand, our casualties in the last week have been nil. That doesn't disappoint me any. Maybe it's do to [with] the fact that the boys have learned to keep their heads down and stay under cover, because, since the 1st three or four weeks, our percentage of casualties has cut down within the Platoon. By this time I know well almost everybody within the Platoon, and it's just one big happy family.

Boy, that would really be swell if you get a new garage put up. Just trying to keep up with the neighbors, hey? It would have to be a fast job to get it up before winter.

I've enclosed a couple of communist propaganda leaflets. They attach them to mortar shells and fire them into our lines and, when the shell lands, the leaflets fly all over. They show how well we would be treated if we would let them take us prisoner. I got news for them—forget it!

Love, Dick

Hi Mom and Dad,   December 2, 1952

I have been rather busy moving back to a reserve area after 49 days on the front lines. Just think, in three more days we will have completed two months over here. It feels good to be able to hit the rack (sleeping bag) nights without having to worry about dashing out to treat some casualty.

It appears to be a nice reserve area, and all us corpsmen (seven) from Fox Company stay in a big tent with two stoves. We have our own racks and plenty of room to store our gear.

I was over to see Jerry yesterday, had a long conversation, and compared letters. Easy Company is on one side of the camp and Fox on the other. We get hot chow and evening movies, so you can see it's just like home compared to the front lines. Chances are that we will remain in a reserve area through Xmas and New Years.

Until I spoke with Jerry, I didn't know we had made HM3. Somehow he got the word, and I am glad to hear it. I also heard that Bobby Day (and several other boys we know that were in Class 46) got rear line jobs with outfits that never get far enough up front to see, smell, or hear old "Luke the Gook."

Jerry received seven letters, two from you, one from Skip Koba, the Kent folks, Grandma and Donald Baird. And he got one from Skip Maur that was addressed to me. Jerry got his box from you by Thanksgiving, but mine didn't make it. We did both receive boxes from Norman and Ethel Hill. I received a letter from Virgil saying his girl Joan is in Japan. She wants to see him because she thinks she's in love with some other guy and wants to be sure she doesn't love him anymore.

Here's the dope on the safety-glass jackets you asked about. We call them "flak jackets." They're number one and everybody has to wear them while on the front line. They knock down a lot of our corpsmen's business. I can think of at least five men right within my own platoon that may have been killed or badly wounded had they not worn them.

Back in World War II the Army developed flak jackets, but they were only worn as an experiment. Somehow the Army believed them to be of little value and quite heavy, so it wasn't until the Marines started wearing them during this Korean deal that the Army finally realized their great value. As far as heaviness, you would be surprised how light they get when the mortar shrapnel starts flying. I'm so used to mine, it's like putting on another shirt.

Jerry with helmet, flak jacket, and mustache—Third Platoon, Easy Company, Second Battalion, "Fighting Fifth," First Marine Division

Our troops will spend daytime digging trenches, which means one of our platoon corpsmen has to accompany them. Still, that gives us every other day off instead of every day on.

Love, Dick

Dear Ma and Pa, December 7, 1952

Here's how I figure my monthly pay now: $122 basic, $45 combat, and about $12 overseas. $10 comes out for insurance, but no income tax. $80 will come home for my allotment, and, occasionally, I'll send even more. I'm sending $100 and $50 dollar money orders home. I must have about $1300 in the bank.

While in Battalion Reserve, our main job is digging. If we dig during the day, we go up to the "Wyoming" line which is a secondary trench line of defense a ways behind the MLR. It is used if the main line is overrun or broken through. My platoon has gone out for eight days in a row and they are getting tired of it. The trench where they are digging is partially in rock, so we have had the assistance of some demolitions men to blast away at the rock. Most of the time I sit around and take care of the fire. We build fires so that the guys can take breaks to warm up during the colder days. When I got up this morning there were two inches of snow on the ground. It's about time, December and all.

Love, Jerry

Dick with a Thompson submachine-gun

Hi Mom and Dad,   December 9, 1952

I received your Xmas box the other day and everything was greatly enjoyed! The little fruitcake came through in wonderful shape, as did everything else. Thanks a lot for the medical dictionary. It's number one, easy to pack around because its both light and reasonably small.

I am sending home pictures taken while we were out digging and others while back on the front line. The one gun I have in my hand (while standing up) is a Thompson Submachine gun. It's a nice little gadget to have when "Luke the Gook" comes around. The other gun that I am sitting behind is a .50 caliber machine gun. It has firepower that the Gooks never like to see fired at them.

The other 3 pictures are showing me treating a casualty. The one group picture is of fellows in the 3rd fire team of one of our platoon squads. McKay has a BAR (Browning Automatic Rifle). The Marines feel it is one of their best weapons.

The temperature is getting down into the 20s at night. In the pictures, notice the snow and the cap with fur-lined ear flaps that can be tied on top

Dick with medical
equipment

or let down over the ears. I had a sweater, two wool shirts, and my gloves on that day.

The bag in the photo that hangs from my shoulder by a strap is our individual unit one medical kit. In it we carry battle dressings, bandages, Morphine, cough medicine, APC pills, shears, EMTS (Emergency Medical Tags), and all kinds of miscellaneous gear like iodine. I have a bottle of Serum Albumin taped onto one of the straps.

Love, Dick

Dear Mom and Dad,   December 18, 1952

Boy, loads of wonderful boxes of goodies have come in in the last 10 days. Let me list them: two from you, one from Norman and Ethel Hill (candy and cookies), the Rossows (cookies), Freedom Grandpa and Grandma (cookies and candies), Uncle Frank and Aunt Lila Gregg (nuts), Martha and Alvin Carson (candy), and Kent Aunts Frances and Louise Hoskins (candy and cookies). All very good. It's kept me busy writing thank you letters.

I also received your letter with the fine pictures of you, which I'm taking as a hint you want more pictures sent home. Well, I sent some film home today (16 pictures) in a little box. Let me know if you get it, and make two sets of the large size.

The last three days the troops have stayed in for classes, so us corpsmen have had it easy.

Jerry's been transferred to another company and I haven't heard from him since.

Love, Dick

Dear Ma and Pa,   December 23, 1952

Well things happen pretty fast in the Marines too. Last Friday night I came in from the field and was given the word that I had been transferred to the 3rd platoon of How ["H"] Company in the 3rd Battalion/5th Regiment along with Knowles and Carey in my company. It's a pretty good platoon. How Company is on the MLR, but will leave the hill and pull back tomorrow night with the rest of the Battalion into regimental reserve after a 3-day exercise. This battalion was way behind in their rotation, so something had to be done. I relieved a kid who was a 22nd drafter. I've gotten in two patrols and two ambushes, with no Gook contact. At least I'll get my combat pay for this month.

Guess what, they have a 16th drafter (I think his name is Krueger) in this Company who lives on Riddle Street in Ravenna, Ohio. He says his dad used to have a dairy store beside the Ravenna theater. He graduated with Darel Porter and went with one of the Jennings girls. I only had a brief talk with him in that he came running down to my bunker yesterday with a piece of shell fragment in his leg, his 3rd purple heart. I may see him in the rear, because anybody who gets three purple hearts doesn't have to put in any more MLR time.

So far they haven't transferred my mail over yet. Several corpsmen are scheduled to replace corpsmen from this platoon, including me. I'm here because the new guys have to have had seven days on the line before they can go in front of the MLR, that is, to an outpost or on a raid.

Now it's the 23rd, and since I haven't got this letter off, I'm adding to it. The night of the 20th we were relieved by Baker ["B"] Company of the 7th Marines. We marched for about a mile down the hill and then sat in some trucks for five hours just waiting. It started raining and then turned to snow. When we finally hit the Wyoming line it was 0430. I carried a stretcher and used it for a rack, but still almost froze for the night was a chiller. Most of the guys slept in the snow. We stayed there the next day and night. We rode by helicopter from the Wyoming line to the Kansas line, slept there the next night in our tents, and then marched four miles to the reserve area.

Grame, Holt, Franklin and four other guys from my Field Medical Class are now relieved to go back to the 3rd Bn/5th Regiment Battalion Aid Station.

Some time tomorrow I'll be sent back to 2nd Bn/5th Reg. Aid Station where I think they are holding my mail. Hope so, because I'll have some packages and letters for Xmas. p.s. "Happy Xmas and New Year."

Love, Jerry

Reflections

DICK: One key point comes to mind. In all the letters dealing with the war, we had to keep our letters to the folks on the light side so that our reports wouldn't scare the daylights out of them. For example, here's what really happened when we first arrived for frontline duty. Both Jerry and I wondered what was up when we were beckoned to the headquarters tent for a chat with the chief petty officer in charge. He said to us something like, "I can see you guys are twins, and I know that so far you have been kept together, but I recommend separating you here, putting you in different companies." When we did not particularly react one way or another, he went on, "Since we've had all the men from entire companies knocked off over here at the same time, it's smart to separate brothers. We can't make you split up, but it's a smart thing to do. It's your decision." Well, we split up mighty fast.

I have a couple of true "war stories" to add here. I omitted them from my letters to the folks because I didn't want to worry them. The first incident has to do with my treating a wounded marine on the front line. Our platoon position consisted of several squads of marines manning sandbag trenches along about 150 yards of the ridge of a hill. One day, just after finishing breakfast, I received word that one of our marines had been wounded at the other end of the line. Because the bunker was near the left end of the line and the wounded guy was at the other end, I had to race through the whole length of the trench line to get to him. Early on I apparently showed too much helmet above the top of the trench, because all the way I kept hearing the zing of snipers' bullets hitting sandbags. Several times (where the trench dipped down into low spots) I jumped out and over the sandbags to cut the distance and save time. It probably wasn't the smartest thing I've ever done, but on that day it worked. When I reached the wounded marine, I was glad to see that it wasn't a serious injury. He had been hit in the arm by shrapnel from an incoming mortar round. I treated the wound, applied antibacterial powder, and patched him up with a battle dressing. Later, it occurred to me that I had made that wild dash without even knowing the extent of the injury.

The other incident involved probably the worst experience I had while serving on the front lines. I grabbed my medical gear and a stretcher as a marine guided me to the location of a reported casualty. It was dark and difficult to see, but we finally reached him.

Much to my surprise, it was one of my fellow corpsmen, Fine. He had a bad upper-leg injury that required two large battle dressings and a shot of morphine. Applying the dressings and giving the shot was tough, because there was so little light. I was able to stop the bleeding, but corpsman Fine was unable to walk; he was pretty well incapacitated. I knew the injury was serious enough to require surgery by a doctor. That meant hauling him back about a mile to the battalion aid station. In the meantime, the marine had brought three Korean civilian workers to help me transport Fine. The marine went back to his position and left me to evacuate him.

Well, the next hour (at least it seemed that long) was very exhausting. The four of us, each lugging a handle of the stretcher, worked our butts off traveling over very rough terrain in the dark, constantly lifting the ends of the stretcher up and down as we crossed rocky and uneven ground. Several of the Koreans got so tired they wanted to quit. I kept them moving. My own arms felt like they were going to fall off from exhaustion. My back was getting tired, too, and I had to keep checking to see how Fine was doing, while making sure he didn't fall off the stretcher.

Needless to say, it was pure joy when I finally saw the BAS. The doctor went to work on Corpsman Fine within minutes. I thanked the Koreans and headed back to my platoon, aware that my unit would be without a corpsman until I got back. Believe me, I had no trouble sleeping that night. Later I heard that Fine recovered okay.

The Thompson submachine gun that I'm displaying in the photo on page 71 has terrific stopping power (firing a fat .45-caliber slug), but its range is limited to about a hundred yards. The "Tommy gun" weighs a little over ten pounds, accepts a magazine of thirty rounds, and fires rapidly. Because it is a short, easily maneuverable weapon, it was popular for night fighting.

The mixture of weapons carried by the thirteen-member marine squads was relatively set. Ten guys lived with their .30-caliber M-1 rifles, which were semiautomatic—that is, eight successive squeezes of the trigger emptied the clip. They too weighed about ten pounds, and their accurate range was about five hundred yards. Three men each carried the squad's most formidable weapon, the .30-caliber BAR (Browning automatic rifle). The squad's three fire teams were built around those twenty-pound portable machine guns, which could fire over five hundred rounds per minute about six hundred yards.

Lieutenants, some staff sergeants, radiomen, and we corpsmen usually carried a holstered .45-caliber revolver and a .30-caliber M-2 carbine. The carbine met our need for a light, relatively short-barreled weapon that could fire rapidly and automatically (thirty rounds).

JERRY: Being on the front line with the marines was certainly a major experience of my life. I had seen enough war movies to know that they were the elite fighting troops of the world, so of course there was a thrilling aspect to being attached to them. With the exception of a few severe incidents, such as our company commander's being killed, I joined them during a relatively quiet period, which was fine with me. I believe it was the commander of Easy Company whom I discuss in my letter of November 12, 1952, who was hit by mortar fire. He led a reinforced platoon patrol in a successful attack on an enemy hill that was defended by a reinforced company. Over a dozen of the enemy were killed, and many were wounded. Only one marine was killed in the attack, but as the patrol returned to the MLR, three rounds of mortar fire killed three more marines and the commander.

Once assigned to my platoon, the members, each in turn, found a way to "drop in" and get to know me, if only to size me up. As I got to know them, some shared war stories with me about the rough engagements they had fought only a few months before I joined them. I liked what I saw and heard about the people and the combat organization. They seemed to realize that we corpsmen (seven per platoon) were—and they wanted and expected us to be—medically trained rather than combat trained. Our role was to get there—as courageously as necessary—to save their lives should they be wounded. They did, of course, expect us to use our revolver and carbine in defense of ourselves and of whatever unit we marched with.

Beyond the care of everyone when in the trenches on the MLR, I had favorite squads whom I preferred to cover on outposts and patrols when it was my turn to go out. Those squads had seasoned men, lead by squad leaders exuding what I perceived to be the right qualities: they were intelligent, soft-spoken, tough, confident, experienced professionals. Such leaders naturally orchestrated effective offensive maneuvers and defensive dispositions. When moving a patrol through no-man's-land on a moonless night or setting up an ambush, the squad leaders positioned me, along with the radioman, protectively, in a nice central spot with plenty of firepower around us. In so doing, they also placed me at an equal distance from the farthest potential casualties.

The size and purpose of a night patrol varied. A reconnaissance patrol could be as small as a ten-man squad, along with a lieutenant, corpsman, and radioman. Larger ambush and contact patrols could consist of two twenty-six-man platoons, a machine-gun unit, three corpsmen, and several radiomen. The Second Battalion, Fifth Marines, at the front usually sent out six patrols every night, and the assignments were rotated among the companies. The no-man's-land between our trenches and those of the enemy was most often small hills flanked by flat valleys covered with rice paddies.

The patrol would slip in single file through a removable section of the wire entanglement protecting our trenches on the MLR. At the edge of the rice paddy, we would form a column and move across no-man's-land. The larger patrols consisted of two parts: a base or fire platoon, with the machine-gun unit, which would set up as we approached our target to cover the enemy; then the second platoon, the assault group, would pass through and attack the outpost or segment of the enemy MLR looming before it. Sometimes we had to wait for a preraid barrage to blast away or for the radioman to request artillery fire. If the artillery blast or enemy flares illuminated our position, all we could do was hit the ground and wait until the glare subsided. The machine-gun units could give the enemy a good licking, but they also drew a lot of attention from the Chinese.

During an ambush or contact patrol, any sign of noise or life from the enemy, even the chatter of one "burp gun," would prompt every marine to open up. I always worried that my glasses would fall off in a firefight and that, being blind as a bat, I would be rendered useless. If we had to sit still for several hours in ambush, it was hard to keep our limbs from turning numb.

On winter nights it seemed we never dressed quite right. If we put on long johns, a flannel shirt, an armored vest, a field jacket, thermal boots, a helmet, and gloves, we were too hot when we were moving along and too cold when sitting in ambush on icy ground.

Many of the larger patrols took along a team of Korean stretcher bearers. Although stretcher units were vital to the evacuation of the wounded, I always thought they made an obvious target, with four men in standing position carrying a six-foot litter. It was a challenge to treat a wounded marine on a stretcher as it moved along rough terrain. I was always impressed that our patrol leader got us back to the right spot on our MLR, for all trails, hills, and rice paddies looked (on a moonlit night) and felt (on a pitch-dark night) the same to me.

I never viewed myself as a "conscientious objector," but I shared the spirit of one. I believe I would have used my weapons in self-defense had I needed to, but I never felt I was there to kill the North Koreans or Chinese. Fortunately, we escaped any sizable, bloody shootouts in our hikes through no-man's-land on contact patrols. The idea was that we were not to return to the MLR until we had captured or killed some of the enemy, even if it meant not returning until into the daylight hours. The barbed-wire incident described in the letter of November 12 is a good example of how the contact patrols I was on were lucky each time.

I often prayed the enemy would stay warm and safe in their bunkers drinking hot coffee or cocoa when my ambush patrol was awaiting them, swatting mosquitoes in the dark of the night. Afterward, if we returned to the MLR without making contact, I was pleased we had failed to lure the enemy into a trap. In my role as a corpsman, my focus was on keeping the injured alive. My concentration was on ensuring life, not liquidating it, and that philosophy gave me a purpose and a tolerance for being there.

Along the trenches, from bunker to bunker, there was always much discussion as to what the marines were doing in Korea. What was our goal, our job? Defensively, we guessed we were to "hang out" on the MLR to stop any major "jump off" or enemy advance into South Korea. We were there to counterattack against smaller (battalion or company-sized) attempts to overrun outposts or penetrate our MLR, and to harass their patrol movements with patrols of our own. The corpsmen also had to contend with sniper casualties when individual marines got too relaxed on the MLR.

Offensively, perhaps the status of the truce talks, while I was on the line, kept the higher-level command from ordering our whole company, or even my platoon, against one of the enemy's strongholds (that is, outpost or hill). I do have to mention the difference I perceived between myself and a fellow platoon corpsman who shared a bunker with me. I wanted to avoid life-taking confrontations as much as possible, while he seemed to thrive on them. Mac was physically and mentally tougher than most of the marines in our platoon. He always implied that a rugged Akron, Ohio, background—possibly mob related—motivated him to be in the heart of dangerous situations and action.

Mac often met in our bunker with some of the tougher marines to exchange impressive hometown battle stories and talk fight strategies. His tales often matched those of even the most outstanding, "gung-ho" marine of the platoon, named something like "Geronimo," from the streets of New York.

On several occasions when I was scheduled to go out on a contact patrol where a bloody battle seemed imminent, he would bribe or plead with me to swap turns and let him go out in my place. When Mac went out on patrol or had duty on an outpost, he would borrow a submachine gun to carry, most often his favorite, a "grease gun." The incident I report in the letter of November 12 in which a platoon was hit hard while out on an outpost, with Mac in the center of the action, could well have been one of those swap occasions. Well, any way you look at it, I was always plenty glad to have Mac around, as well as all those tough marines.

Our bunkers were situated on the reverse slope of the ridge, out of sight from the enemy trenches. Most bunkers had a Yukon stove for heat and some light cooking, and candles for light. They had thick wooden supporting beams, sandbag walls and beds, a crude wooden table, and lots of photos of beautiful women taped to the beams. Showers of dirt fell each time a shell landed anywhere nearby. We had to sleep on raised structures (sandbags) against the wall, because all the bunkers had rats. The space (ranging from a hundred to a thousand yards) between our MLR and that of the Chinese was no-man's-land.

We were certainly glad we had our flak jackets and that all the marines faithfully wore theirs. Those lightweight nylon combat vests contained slabs of glass-cloth filaments, bonded together under heavy pressure. When they were worn, wounds that might have been fatal or serious became light, and light wounds became bad bruises. These "bullet-proof" vests were no better than paper against rifle or machine-gun fire, but they could stop most grenade, mortar, and artillery fragments, as well as bullets from submachine guns, pistols, and other low-velocity firearms. The overall reduction in U.S. casualties due to flak jackets was estimated at from 50 to 70 percent.

The key experience we all shared was time spent on outposts. Such duty was never much fun. There was always the fear of unexplained noises and movements from down the draw, or gully, where the garbage was thrown. Empty C-ration cans tossed down into the gullies and ravines leading to the outpost made the footing very unstable and cut down the chance of a sneak attack. But when the cans clattered in the dark, you never knew when it was the Chinese or just the rats foraging for food. Flies, rats, garbage, and fecal waste all contributed to the unbearable stench.

The other event that got a lot of discussion was Dwight D. Eisenhower's visit to Korea. Letters from our folks had kept us posted on the 1952 presidential election campaign. They felt that General Eisenhower was the best bet. He would find a way to end the Korean War and stop the bloodshed. In November 1952 about thirty-four million Americans went to the polls and voted him in to lead the nation. We never saw the general when he kept his promise in December to visit Korea, but he did show up and survey the scene. He went away convinced that the course pursued by the Truman administration was sound. The word was that he put on field gear, went out and talked to, and ate rations with, some of the troops, and watched an artillery barrage.

Chapter Six

Battalion Aid Stations

$\mathcal{D}$uring this two-month (January and February 1953) phase of our rotation scheme, we were assigned to several battalion aid stations. Once we moved to positions behind the MLR, our daily life became far less threatening. The number of casualties remained low, because of such factors as the winter weather, the on-and-off truce talks, and the early negotiations for exchange of prisoners of war. In addition, Lt. Gen. Maxwell D. Taylor, who succeeded General Van Fleet as Eighth Army commander in February, issued directives that helped reduce casualties. He stressed the need to plan and rehearse patrols, to provide complete eight-week training programs for reserve divisions before they reentered the line, and for troops to use better concealment measures when on skylines.

The Second Battalion, Fifth Marines, returned to the MLR on 23 January 1953, to defend the right-battalion sector of the rightmost regiment of the First Marine Division; we remained in the battalion aid stations. Most of the casualties we now received and treated were wounds from mortar and artillery fire (which had been considerably reduced during the winter lull), small-arms fire (rifles, machine guns, and grenades) during patrol action, and stepping on mines. There was always sharp fighting, day and night, somewhere along the line. All the squads and platoons took turns moving out to capture, kill, and dislodge the enemy, and they always invited a corpsman along. These events brought a number of individual and small-group casualties into the battalion aid stations.

Letters

Dear Mom and Dad,   December 24, 1952

"Happy New Year." We have moved from Battalion Reserve Camp to Division Reserve camp. Between locations we spent 24 hours on the secondary Kansas trench line. Tonight is Xmas eve and I will go over to my favorite squad and help them throw a big party.

I have good news that will be a Christmas present for you. I've been transferred back to Battalion Aid Station (BAS) and thus am no longer in Fox Company. It's the first step back from being a front line platoon corpsman. Jerry's outfit is now also back in reserve and he should be joining me here shortly.

The BAS corpsmen help the doctors hold sick call here in reserve, and when up on the lines they aid the doctors to treat casualties after the platoon corpsmen have patched up the wounded and moved them away from the point of action.

Just received two big boxes from Grandma Richardson filled with swell canned fruits. One is Jerry's, so I'm saving it for him.

Glad to hear that you have finished building the garage. I hope you can get it painted soon.

Guess what? Another corpsman (Brocker) and I went out, cut, set up, and decorated a Xmas tree and have it looking sharp. The only thing is, it's for the officers.

I've got things to do, so will sign off for now.

Love, Dick

Dear Ma and Pa,   December 29, 1952

When I was still back in 3rd Bn/5th Reg Christmas Eve, we practically had a 25th draft reunion. About ten of the guys I know from the 7th Marines came over, including Holt. Late in the afternoon we sang Xmas carols with some of the Korean Marines. The next day three of us were transferred back to 2nd Bn/5th Reg. in time for a good Xmas meal.

Here at Battalion Aid Station there are four of us on duty each day. At 0830 we have sick call with two doctors (usually for about 50 Marines). For a couple of hours we are really busy giving shots, passing out APCs, etc. Then the rest of the day is usually quiet, for back here in reserve there are

Dick and Jerry with ambulance jeep

Dick with jeep driver Ellis and corpsman Al Fine

Jerry in front of the battalion aid station tent

The batallion mess hall and movie theater, with marines in line for chow

HM3 (Corpsman Third Class)
Bill Brocker

seldom any casualties. Today we did have 80 for sick call. Since my duty is mostly to give shots, I've given more in the last week than in all my past naval career.

There is one big tent for sick call and another one for our living quarters. They are close to the movie tent and chow hall, so I've got no complaints.

Your films came just at the right time, because both Dick and I were lucky enough to get the first BAS liberty to Seoul, Korea, along with two truck loads of Marines, Dr. Henry, MacGowan, and three other corpsmen. It was a cool ride for a couple of hours until we arrived in town at 10:30. We were on our own for the afternoon to see the city. It was an interesting trip. Most of the people wear pants except for some of the old *Mama-sans*. We snapped two rolls of film on the Korean people alone.

Seoul was interesting, but the city is all bombed up. They tell us it has changed hands about 10 times. Most of the people are shy (except the kids) and we had quite a time getting them to let us take their pictures.

I hope you folks are ready to start the New Year off with a bang. The weather is pretty cool here with snow flurries every once in a while.

Love, Jerry

Jerry enjoying a Seoul, Korea, street scene

Hi Mom and Dad,   December 31, 1952

Well, this year has just about had it. It will seem funny putting the 3 in back of the 5. Two days ago I received quite a few Xmas cards (the McBrides, Coburns, Kobas, Dudaks, Hills, and Hoskins) plus another big box from you. Thanks for the socks, film, and candles. Your homemade cookies were just swell. Only one trouble—not enough (ha)!

Our trip to Seoul was fun. As soon as we got off the truck there were about 15 Korean kids running around and pestering us to death. While most wanted to shine our shoes or show us around, some wanted to fix us up with their sister for a date. Some of them just won't take no for an answer. Every time I took a step, I had another black streak across one shoe and a red streak across the other. If you stopped for a minute, about four kids would be there putting one of your feet on a shoeshine box. Some fun. We didn't know whether to laugh or get annoyed. Jerry and I solved the problem by hopping on a bus and riding to the other side of town. The 32 snaps I'm sending home will

Doctor Henry with a Seoul shoeshine boy

give you a good idea of what the people are like. You see a lot of the women cooking food on the sidewalks of the streets.

For the last five "off duty" days I have been running down to the regimental dentist to have work done on my teeth.

Our BAS handles men from Fox, Easy, Dog, and Weapons companies. There are 12 corpsmen here including Jerry and the Chief in Charge. Our chances of going back to a line company are slim now, unless something big breaks.

Glad to hear you got my recent $150 to the bank. Have to run to chow.

Love, Dick

Dear Ma and Pa, January 2, 1953

My mail finally caught up with me, five letters from you, five Xmas cards, your number 1 pictures, and your second air mail box with candles, cookies, dates, marshmallows, and fruit. We've never received any goodies that haven't hit our stomachs in a hurry.

My glasses are broken in a couple of places, so I need to go back for a new pair one of these days. Although President Eisenhower didn't come to our unit, we heard that he did visit Korea. As far as Douglas MacArthur goes, I don't think I'd listen to him too long.

We learned that there was a big celebrity show in Seoul, including Ravenna's own Peggy King, that we missed by a day or two. Did receive a letter from Russell Tisher who's over here (in charge of a shower unit) and he got to see the Peggy King Show along with Debbie Reynolds. Guess Peggy found out he was there from Ravenna, called him out of the audience, and sang a couple of songs for him, plus called him back stage for a talk later.

Love, Jerry

Hi Mom and Dad,   January 11, 1953

I've enclosed some pictures from a fellow marine that illustrate the type of landscape over here. There's a shot of a portion of the famous Bunker Hill. It's right in back of the darkest ridge near the sky and looks like a cloud because its white in color due to being bombed so much. Our position while on line was to the right of Bunker Hill. There is one of the Company C.P. area (which was located about ¼ mile back of the MLR), one of a First Aid Bunker near it, and one showing the Gook territory across from our position while on line. The hills and rice paddy terrain look peaceful, but believe me it wasn't. Siberia, which is across the rice paddy on the left, was where our combat patrols made most of their contacts with the Gooks. They have a big trench system running all along Siberia.

The lighter-appearing hill in the rear is No Name Ridge. Our planes used to bomb it quite regularly and we got to see some wonderful air attacks. The tree-covered area across the rice paddy and in the right portion of the picture was our forward outpost (Samoa). The only way we could send men out there was by crossing the rice paddy and that could only be done at night. Between the other five company corpsmen and myself, we had *tak-a-san* (many) casualties on that position.

There are two pictures of Napalm bombs dropped by U.S. planes. The Gooks used to throw in the big gear [artillery attacks] around the bunker that is along our own MLR. The Marine's marking of "61 and 82 alley" means that's where the Gooks used to drop in all their 61 mm. and 82 mm. mortar shells.

The 28th draft came in yesterday and we got three corpsmen for this Bn out of the deal. We really get a kick out of telling the new guys how rough it is in the field (ha). Until a corpsman actually sees the MLR, he is usually shaking in his boots. This makes about 18 days we have been with BAS and time has sure been moving right along.

Yes, now Jerry and I will probably remain together.

Today I received your wonderful box that came in last night. Thanks a million!

Well I've got to run to chow, so will close for now.

Love, Dick

Dear Ma and Pa, January 12, 1953

We've been in Korea about 3 months and a week. We are now attached to Battalion Aid which is under the Headquarters and Service Company of the 2nd Battalion/5th Regiment. Our sick calls [that is, the numbers of men attending sick call] are cutting down quite a bit now, must be the Marines are getting used to the cold weather. The word has come out for Bn Quarterly Shots, so that's about all we will be doing for a while.

This seems to be a number one reserve camp. We are seeing a lot of movies and playing cards. In case I never mentioned it, I've been using the tea bags you sent, right along. Taste pretty good on a cold night.

The way things are set up here, each battalion is off by itself and doesn't get too much news from other places. Unless we go back to regiment or over to visit somebody, we don't hear the latest word.

In the articles from the "Stars and Stripes" I've sent home, you can see Bunker Hill which is right on the 38th parallel. Panmunjom, the peace area below it, has an outpost three miles out in front of the MLR. The hook north of it is the hot spot that was overrun where many Marines were killed. Today it got warm enough for us to play some football.

Love, Jerry

Hi Mom and Dad, January 23, 1953

For the last four nights it has been down below zero. This morning when we got up both stoves in our tent had gone out and liquid containers nearby had ice on them. I usually sleep in a sleeping bag in my longies with a blanket thrown over me.

Finally got a letter from Bobby Day saying he's getting along well (1st Battalion, 1st Marines) and will soon be relieved back to BAS. He was up on line right along, including being out in an outpost. We are due to move back up on the line with the Battalion.

We've been giving shots (Typhoid, Typhus, Cholera, Cowpox, Influenza and Tetanus) for seven days. Knocked off H and S [Headquarters and Service], Weapons, Easy, Dog, and Fox Companies. Those poor Marines (ha).

Here are a couple of pictures Bill Brocker took and gave to me. Albertson, the big Salt Lake Mormon of the 25th draft, stopped in to see us.

Got to sign off for today and write some more letters.

Love, Dick

Dear Ma and Pa,   January 26, 1953

H. and S. Company and the Bn have moved back where there is little action and now we don't even have to wear flak jackets. We have been put on a three-section-watch [rotation], one day on duty, next day stand-by for ambulance runs, and next day off completely. We have half of a Quonset hut for sick call and a fortified bunker for casualties. Good set up. No movies though, tough.

The days we've had the duty have been quiet most of the time. We get up about 0700 and work until 2100 [9 P.M.], but the sick call is *skochi* (small) and most of the time we just sit by the phone. I had a small casualty from Dog Company and Dick took care of a Korean "Chogie-bearer" that got hit in the thigh.

We have only 180 guys here at Battalion Headquarters so the chow is Number One. Our hospital bunker is solid wood supported by five layers of sandbags. It's probably the safest spot in the regimental area, if something would break out. We usually have a few guys with the grippe or flu which we hold until they get better.

Still got the same old taped-up glasses, but should get new ones any day. Frank Leonard finally wrote. Received a letter from Kenny Kline who is now stationed near Tokyo, Japan. Says he will be there till he gets discharged about two years from now. Wow!

Had ice cream again tonight for chow. That's one good thing about the Marines, the colder it gets, the more ice cream they give us.

Love, Jerry

Hi Mom and Dad,   January 29, 1953

After 10 dental visits I have a set of teeth, including a bridge and $55 worth of gold fillings.

Today is our 6th day in our new position, and we like it. We get a shower every 3rd day plus a changie-changie on clothes. When on standby, we make runs after casualties. We see about everything, e.g., I've brought back a Korean worker hit by accident with a hand grenade and a Marine with an injury caused by an exploding stove.

I'm sending home six rolls of film, some pictures of our old reserve home, of tanks, of my old platoon in a reserve maneuver, and of weapons (61 mortars and the 75 mm recoilless).

We've received Ray Zbornick's box of nuts, Grandma Richardson's letter and picture of Marilyn Marks and her two kids (Jeff and Cheryl), Bobby Day's letter saying he's now back at regiment, and Frank's letter reporting that he is back in college and that Paul Collins is engaged. That's another classmate that's about to tie the knot. So Ronnie Newcome has a girlfriend. Yes, we do remember Virginia, but did not know her well.

Love, Dick

Dear Mom and Dad,   February 2, 1953

Things have been exciting the past 2 days as we have been quite busy fulfilling our role as corpsmen. Easy Company went on a night raid. While the bulk of the corpsmen stood by here at BAS with one doctor, Jerry and another doctor went up to a forward aid position on the MLR. Luckily, when Easy Company made contact with the Gooks there were only two slight casualties. However, at approximately the same time the Lt. of Fox Company, that was out on patrol, got hit by a bullet. So one of our jeep drivers and two corpsmen took off to help him, applied battle dressings, and brought him back to the aid station where the doctor determined the injury to be serious. To combat the loss of blood, we quickly gave the Lt. seven bottles of Serum Albumin and one bottle of plasma. A helicopter had already been sent for and was landing to evacuate him. Within minutes we put him in a protective evacuation bag, loaded him on the copter, and sent him back for major surgery at one of the medical companies. We could see that the bullet had entered his hip and then passed upward into the abdomen. We learned later when we got a report back that it went clear up through his diaphragm into a lung. Turned out, that although they had to surgically remove his spleen, a kidney and part of his intestines, he was still alive and holding his own.

On the morning of the 31st, Dog Company was scheduled to pull a big daytime raid on a Gook hill. Two of us corpsmen (myself and Johnson), plus a doctor, went up to a forward aid position and stood by with medical gear, anticipating that there could be a number of casualties. Our preparation paid off, because before the morning was over we had treated (with the help of the platoon corpsman on the raid) about 24 Marine casualties. And Dog Company was lucky to have had only that few wounded. Unfortunately, there were two KIAS (killed in action) and two other Marines had serious injuries—one with a penetrating lung wound and one with a bad leg wound and fractures. About six of the wounded were evacuated by copter and the rest by our ambulance jeeps. The platoon corpsmen were lucky to have been among the unwounded.

I also got word that my old platoon outfit with Fox Company had been hit on a patrol four nights earlier. Four of the fellows I had gotten to know well during my three months duty with them, plus one other fellow, were all killed. Another fellow I knew, plus the corpsman, were also badly wounded. They evacuated the two wounded out by helicopter.

Needless to say, being on a contact patrol against the Gooks just isn't the safest place to be. Our Battalion Aid Station is about 1 mile back of the MLR, so we never get any incoming mortar shells or have to worry about sniper bullets like the platoon corpsmen on the line do.

Well I must sign off for tonight.

Love, Dick

Dear Ma and Pa,   February 7, 1953

We've been over here about four months. That's racking up a quarter of a year in a hurry. I knocked off the cake you sent. Tasted good, really fresh.

Well, a few things happened a week ago. About 7 nights back I went up to Easy Company's C.P. with Doctor Henry to set up a forward aid bunker, because the company was pulling a reinforced patrol raid. Somehow they managed to complete the raid with nothing more than a couple of white-phosphorous burns for casualties. Our efforts were not in vain though, because one of the platoons on the MLR had some casualties from incoming mortar shells.

The next morning Dog Company pulled a daylight raid involving 95 men. We had three corpsmen, including Dr. Colston, up at a forward aid bunker and the rest of us back here waiting at BAS. We used three armored personnel carriers (vehicles something like tanks) to carry the casualties from forward aid to Bn aid. Dick was up at forward aid and he said the casualties started coming in at about 0830.

Dog Company got off lucky in that, when it was all over, they had gotten up to the Gook trenches and killed quite a few Gooks. Everything went smoothly from a military point of view. Odd as it may seem, the Marines considered the raid a success in that many more Gooks were killed than Marines. Our losses consisted of having two men killed and about 22 wounded. Only two of the wounded were serious. They were immediately flown out by helicopter.

We have been harassed by the brass lately. Now we have to cover all our bunkers and tents with camouflage. Its about a three day job.

The candles and boxes are coming in handy now, because we don't have any PX or electric lights. The Chaplain gave us a steak the other night and we fried it. A real treat! You could send a little salt in the next box, because it's scarce too. Also a comb.

We got our income tax statements. I made just short of a $1000 last year. Had about $75 withheld. Don't know how much I'll get back.

For the last few days our main occupation has been filling sandbags. I think we have put about a thousand bags on our bunker and only covered two layers, so you can see it is a big one. We put bags about chest high around our sickbay and the doctor's tent. Probably the first hard work I've done since joining the Marines.

A new colored ambulance driver has replaced our old one. He seems like a pretty good guy and has a radio. The music really sounds good in our tent.

It has been like spring or early summer over here lately. We are expecting the 29th draft in sometime this week to relieve the outgoing 17th draft.

We are only having one hot meal a day now—C-rations for the other two.

I got a letter from Skip Maur saying he likes college. He was really snowed when he got his new Nash Rambler as a surprise present.

Love, Jerry

Hi Mom and Dad, February 14, 1953

I received your Valentine and birthday cards. Thanks! Also your picture of the new garage. It looks terrific! Does it have one of those downward sliding doors?

We are still serving the 2nd Battalion, 5th Regiment, 1st Marine Division. Several weeks back our area got about eight rounds of mortar shells. That's why we've been filling sandbags and camouflaging our tents. Regarding the rounds, we decided the Gooks were just testing one of their long-range guns and happened to be aiming in our direction (ha), but some big shot decided we had better wear our flak jackets, helmets, and carry our medical bags.

They have the Marines working 16 hours a day up on the MLR laying barbed wire. Most of the casualties lately have been from guys stepping on mines.

You asked if we were in on any of the big battles. Most of ours were smaller platoon-sized raids. We did have one of our Battalions (the 1st) in the 5th Regiment conduct a big company-sized raid that killed around 350 Gooks. Our Battalion only had 16 KIAs and around 60 casualties. Unfortunately, four of them were corpsmen. A crew from our BAS was on stand-by consisting of Dr. Henry, a jeep ambulance and a corpsman.

Got your newspaper clippings on Peggy King (marriage), classmates Maxine Skilton and Gene Baker, and heard that Jack Chin is going with one of the Smith girls.

Love, Dick

Reflections

JERRY: I remember two incidents while I was on duty at the Battalion Aid Stations that I did not write about in my letters. The first was one of the times they sent BAS corpsmen back to the front line to provide medical help in the absence of, or in addition to, the platoon corpsmen. They sent me to an outpost situated in front of and considerably below our MLR trench line. Several marines carried stretchers while leading me down a steep, rugged, winding trail.

I was concerned that I would never make it down, because it was pitch dark; I had to feel my way while hanging on to an extra load of medical equipment. The word was that the squad of marines manning the outpost had been hit with artillery shell fragments. Reaching the wormlike network of the outpost's trenches, I could hear several marines moaning close by.

It turned out that a number of the marines had shrapnel wounds, but most of them were flesh wounds, which I patched up in a hurry with bandages. None were lost limbs or serious head or chest wounds. However, the marines manning the outpost got nervous at the way I was running around the trenches loudly directing my helpers to evacuate one marine after another. They feared the noise would prompt another round of shells. They also went crazy at my insistence on using my pocket flashlight to check the severity of several shoulder and abdominal wounds. Since my motivation was to save the lives of the marines already injured, I didn't care who heard me or who saw me doing it. I'm sure the marines remaining on the outpost were one happy group when I finally escorted the last casualty back up the cliffside path.

The other incident occurred when I was back at BAS. One of my old squads, which was still on the front line, had incurred casualties by setting off a land mine while on a patrol. We were able to meet the needs of most of the injured and send them back to their trenches and bunkers. But one guy, who had been one of my favorite marines, was not so lucky. Perhaps he was the one who tripped the mine; he had been close to it. His legs were in critical condition, and the attending doctor felt he would lose one leg or both. A helicopter flew him to a nearby hospital.

That night I agonized over how the loss of his legs would affect him psychologically. I decided the only helpful thing I could do was write a consoling letter to him and his parents. I wrote and rewrote most of the night, tearing up each attempt in turn, feeling that it failed to relieve my grief and that it would be of little comfort to him. My letter, as I finally sent it, emphasized how my high school coach, James Whittaker, had survived the loss of a leg. Coach had been an Ohio State track star; he lost a leg in a car accident, was given an artificial leg, and thereafter became a great teacher and coach of several championship teams. Many a time over the years I've thought of that wounded squad member and my feeble attempt to soothe him in a letter. However, I am betting that he did survive, for he was a special marine.

The "Peggy King" referred to in my letters of January 2 and February 14 had graduated from Ravenna Township High School in 1947. She was a successful singer, touring with such top bands as Charlie Spivak, Ray Anthony, and Ralph Flanagan. Thereafter she joined the Mel Torme and George Gobel television shows and appeared on the *Jack Benny Show* and the *Bob Hope Christmas Show*. In 1955 she was nominated for an Emmy as best female singer, and later she performed on the Academy Awards show.

Chapter Seven
Able Medical Company

*T*he letters of this chapter cover our experiences during the final phase of our Korean tour of duty. Rotated back to the rear for service in Able ("A") Medical Hospital, we were both given work assignments in the medical records department. Because our job was that of taking care of health records, at the end of March we were sent to Japan on a liaison team to meet an incoming marine draft and manage their records. Then, in July, we were granted a rest and recuperation leave in Japan.

The *Stars and Stripes* newspaper kept us abreast of the war. As our duty at the hospital continued, the melting snows and mud of spring made roads impassable and streams too swift and deep for crossing. For a while, we were granted a lull in the fighting.

Then the helicopter action increased, bringing casualties to Able Hospital's reception platform, as the Chinese accelerated their tempo on the First Marine Division's front. Dick's letters of March 26 and April 6, 1953, and his comments in the Reflections section, discuss the impact of these outpost battles on the Second Battalion he had served with. The Chinese threw two company-sized attacks against Fifth Marine Regiment outposts. They were beaten off, and the marines quickly counterattacked. Just before our trip to Japan, around the 22nd of March, the Chinese mounted a counterblow, sending two companies against the First Marine Regiment's outposts Hedy and Bunker Hill, just four miles east of Panmunjom. The fighting involved fierce hand-to-hand combat. After several days of surging back and forth, with the fighting continuing all night and fierce artillery bombardments isolating the battleground, the marines reestablished the outpost line and held it fast.

Then, in a surprise attack on March 26, the Chinese Communists launched elements of six companies (over seven hundred men) against marine outposts Carson, Reno, and Vegas, manned by companies of the First and Third Battalions of the Fifth Marines—each outpost defended by forty or fifty men, including two corpsmen. Attacks and counterattacks raged continuously for five days. The enemy encircled the outposts, swarmed into the trenches, and engaged the marines in hand-to-hand combat.

All three platoons of Dick's old Fox Company were dispatched from the Second Battalion reserve to reinforce outpost Reno. Ambushed and bombarded by a constant rain of mortar and artillery fire (casualties in one platoon reached 70 percent in minutes), they fought their way into the trenches and joined Charlie ("C") Company, also depleted. By midnight on the 26th, the dwindling units had fought three more clashes against four attacking Chinese platoons.

During the 27th and 28th of March, Jerry's old Easy Company of Second Battalion, Fifth Marines (or as we would have said, "two-five") and Fox Company of 2/7 attempted to retake outpost Vegas in a savage, ten-hour fight. It was a busy night for marines and corpsmen alike. Easy Company finally retook and held the outpost. Men from Fox Company (2/5) joined up with them; altogether, the ragtag group mustered only five squads—sixty men from Easy Company and eight from Fox. On the 29th and 30th they repelled two attacks in battalion strength within a six-hour period, and the five-day siege ended. Marine casualties totaled over a thousand (over a hundred killed, four hundred seriously wounded and evacuated, and a hundred missing).

My letter of July 8, 1953, refers to the tough, back-and-forth, hand-to-hand fighting that resulted when a reinforced Chinese infantry battalion attacked outposts Berlin and East Berlin, each defended by a platoon of the Seventh Marines, on the night of July 7. The marines lost East Berlin, but they counterattacked and retook it. Both sides delivered heavy artillery and mortar fire (each side threw in about twenty thousand rounds). In the end there were nine marines killed, twelve missing, and 120 wounded and evacuated. Thirty Chinese are known to have been killed, an estimated two hundred were missing, and four hundred wounded.

When we were happily headed for rest and recreation in Japan, we heard that the fireworks of this battle had given even the hospital's corpsmen a scare. Soon after we left, a provisional platoon from our Headquarters and Service Company had been rushed to reinforce the main line, only three hundred yards behind the East Berlin outpost.

Dick's letter of July 28, 1953, refers to this final battle for the Berlin outposts. The clashes started on the night of July 19, when the Chinese threw another major offensive against Berlin and East Berlin outposts and captured them once more. This time the marines unleashed a tank, artillery, mortar, and air attack more powerful than any that had yet been seen. Bombers delivered tons of napalm and other bombs. By the end of the day on July 20, all the outpost bunkers were completely demolished, and all but fifteen yards of trench line on East Berlin had been reduced to rubble. The enemy lost at least seventy-five men killed and three hundred wounded, and their battalion was so worn down by casualties in other sectors that it had to be replaced on the MLR.

On July 24, the Chinese hurled a heavy attack against outpost Esther but failed to break through the Fifth Marines sector. Using tanks, flamethrower tanks, and every other weapon available, the marines drove the Chinese off with heavy casualties. The enemy lost about five hundred men in the assault, while the marines suffered a hundred casualties, including a dozen dead.

By the end of the day on July 27, the Chinese assault, which had extended the entire length of the Eighth Army MLR, had come to an end. In their attempt to overrun the Eighth Army, the enemy had sent in at least six armies (some seventy-five thousand men) along the Iron Triangle, the Punchbowl, and the Kumsong Bulge.

The other situation building in Korea, one that we witnessed at the time of our departure from Korea, was the prisoner of war issue. The *Stars and Stripes* reported that in early April 1953 a POW liaison group had met at Panmunjom, exchanged lists of names, and set a date for what the Americans called Operation Little Switch. It began on April 20, with the Communists returning a hundred a day and the UN five hundred. The final stage in the exchange of prisoners of war began on August 5. The army set up a MASH mobile evacuation hospital to receive litter cases by ambulance. Units from the marines were involved in the reception group, waiting near the Peace Pagoda near Panmunjom with transportation trucks and medical tents for the ambulatory POWs. India was assigned to provide troops to supervise the final exchange, named Operation Big Switch, at a place known as Freedom Village.

Letters

Hi Mom and Dad,   February 16, 1953

Surprise! Now is the time for all good men to come to the aid of their country. Guess what—I can still type. Do you recognize the high school typing drill?

We are now in the rear with the gear and have office jobs. Yesterday we received our orders and were transferred back here to Able Medical Company. It is one of the three Medical Companies (hospitals) attached to the 1st Marine Division (and by far the largest). We are going to work in the Medical Records Section of the Headquarters and Service Company of the 1st Medical Battalion of the 1st Marine Division.

This is some change over Battalion Aid Station, hey! We couldn't have asked for a nicer birthday present. They have movies, electric lights, and fairly decent quarters. It's like an old reunion seeing all the 25th drafters we came over with, because most of them got relieved at the same time.

We did get some bad news about Coy Brewer, a classmate of ours back at [Medical Corps] school. He had also spent eight months with us at Bethesda plus coming over with us on the 25th draft. Coy was in Dog Company of 2nd Bn/5th Reg and I'm sure we have quite a few pictures of him back home. He was killed in a contact patrol shortly after our arrival in Korea. Brewer and three others were the total of KIAS in the 25th corpsman's draft.

Stellwag, the boy from Long Island that we spent the New York weekend with, came over on the 23rd draft and may have lost a leg. I will have to check up on that.

I didn't want to tell you when it happened, but Sammis (the corpsman I worked with first in my old platoon) didn't just get relieved because his time was up. He got wounded in the leg by some incoming mortar shrapnel during the daytime on an outpost. It was good that it wasn't too serious, because it would have been almost impossible to get him off. They were going to send tanks up to pull him out, until he informed them he could hold off till that night. I never got into the act because that night I was out on a patrol with one of our squads. However, he has completely recovered and is now working at Easy Medical Company.

The following will be current for my new change of address: Richard G. Chappell, HM3, 571-80-61, H. and S. Co., 1st Medical Battalion, 1st Marine Division, c/o F.P.O., San Francisco, California.. The duty probably won't be

Jerry standing beside the entrance to the medical hospital

quite as exciting back here as it was at BAS, but it is a little safer (ha). Well I have some other things to square away, so I will sign off for today.

Love, Dick

Dear Ma and Pa,   February 17, 1953

Yes, it was about the quietest birthday I've ever had. I was glad to get the comb, because I was still using Dick's.

We figured that we would get relieved this time, but did not know for sure, so we never said anything about it. The movies and chow back here are the best I have found so far. It is just about like working back at Bethesda Hospital for me. I'm starting to work in Health Records. It's the records for all the corpsmen who are in 1st Medical Battalion. I think it will be a very good job when I get the hang of it. One thing I'll do is check records to see who needs shots. We work from 0800 to 1630 and pull a fire watch about every fourth night. There are quite a few guys back here that we know.

The danger is over for us. It would take a lot of Gooks to ever get back this far and by then we would be in Seoul (ha). They would have to overrun the MLR, the Wyoming Line, the Kansas Line, and swim across the Imjin River before they would get here. It is time to get back to work, so I'd better sign off.

Love, Jerry

Dick with the tent
mascot puppy

Hi Mom and Dad,   February 23, 1953

We are fairly well broken into our new jobs. The following is an average daily schedule: get up at 0645 to catch breakfast, muster at 0730 with a rifle inspection, head for work at 0805 right after colors, knock off work at 1200 till 1245 for chow, knock off for the day at 1630, and go to evening chow (out of this world) about 1700 and a movie at 1900. That's the day's work!

They have me running a mimeograph and graphotype machine. We cut a stencil for anything that the Medical Company's record office or other organizations want run off. Then I run 2–5 hundred copies. I cut dog tags [metal identification tags, worn around the neck] on the graphotype for any Marine unit requesting them.

Our mail started coming in. Received a letter from Russ Tisher and Bruce Patterson who says Jimmy Hudson works at the woolen mill nights and for his dad in the day time. Got the pens from Ray Zbornick and am using one now, the best ballpoint I've ever used. Also, got some wonderful homemade Carmel-nut candy from the Norman Hills for a birthday gift. Next time you see Ethel Hill thank her for us.

I got my first washing done by a *mama-san* from a nearby Korean village. A lot of the fellows take their clothes to these ladies who do the washing right there in a creek. They even have some way to do a number one job of drying and pressing them. For two packs of cigarettes my *mama-san* washed five

Dick pitching horseshoes

pair of socks, 10 handkerchiefs, one set of underwear, one hat, one set of dungarees, and one wool shirt.

Love, Dick

Dear Ma and Pa,   March 23, 1953

The latest word is that four of us are heading for Japan about the 29th. We will meet the incoming load of Marines headed for Korea and work on their Health Records. One of the guys, who has already been over, really knows the ropes and should be able to get us as much liberty as possible.

We got up a small Pinochle tournament and are going to play in the final playoff game. Only four teams are involved, with a case of Tottie [chocolate drink] going to the winner.

You asked about the Health Locator part of my job. It's quite simple. Anybody that gets wounded over here, and goes to one of the hospital ships for treatment, has that part of his record sent onto the outfit that he belongs to, to be entered in his Health Record. Many times he will be transferred two or three times and his records get lost and end up here, so it is my job to write a letter to the Division Health Locator and find out where all these men are and then send the records to the right outfit. If it turns out that there is

HM3 (Corpsman Third Class) Grame with a Korean shoeshine boy and washie-washie women in background

no record of the man over here, I have to send it back to the states for further search.

My typing speed is picking up. I didn't think I would ever get back in the swing again. My new habit is reading novels. Watching some of the other guys read, I realize I have to pick up my reading speed, if I ever want to get through college. I'd like to read something good, so how about sending along three by Mickey Spillane ("Kiss Me Deadly," "The Big Kill," and "Vengeance Is Mine.").

What do you think about Stalin kicking off in March? [Joseph Stalin died of a brain hemorrhage on March 1.] Think it will cause any disturbance in Moscow?

Did I tell you I saw "Swede" Anderson the other day, working on a surgical team which is a different setup over here than FMF? He was my old class adjutant in Corps School. If you get out that picture, he's probably up front and has a big jaw. He's been over here on a surgical team for about 14 months. He informed us that Stellwag did not lose his leg, as we had heard, but only was shot in the leg and is now back stateside. Bobby Day stopped in on a supply run for his regiment and then when he came to pick up his orders. Looks good. He's ending up in Dog Medical Company which we consider the best working place in Korea, as far as hospitals go. Got another letter from the

Kent Aunts, who, next to you, are the most regular. Never say much, but they are regular.

It is raining steady again and our tent leaks around the sides and the water comes in in rivers. The outside detail tent is the worst one around Able Med. and sometimes we get really water logged. No one ever stays in it for over a month, so nobody bothers to fix it up.

Speaking of rivers, let me get you straightened out on the Korean rivers. The Imjin River is the one that Dick took pictures of. A regiment, two battalion reserve areas and all the artillery batteries are located on the other side of the river behind the MLR. On this side we have the big rear outfits, and all the hospitals. We won't be seeing the Yalu River because it is on the other side of "Tate-oc-son" which we consider one of the Gooks strongest points around here [the Yalu River separates North Korea from China]. If you ever hear of the Marines crossing the Yalu River, you can figure they had *taka-san* (many) casualties.

The calves must be growing fast to be having kids already. That's about the latest. Guess I better be heading for the shower and washie-washie.

This will be my last letter until we get to Japan.

Love, Jerry

Hi Mom and Dad,   March 26, 1953

We have received four more wonderful boxes from you and three packages from relatives and neighbors. A letter from Virgil says he is slowly getting tired of Japan. Maybe he's wishing his tour of duty there were shorter. Funny how Kenny, Virgil and the two of us all ended up in the Orient at the same time.

Pankus, the boy we ran around with in California (and some while on the lines) is now back here with us at Able Med. The rumor we heard that he had his head blown off was wrong. Dick Holt was sent to galley duty, Tyson the Admission Desk, Brocker the operation room, and Fine to X-ray in Charlie Medical Company and Bill Kirkland is now in Easy Medical Company.

My old company had another raid and got shot up with 45 casualties, plus five KIAS. However, the bulk of the raiders were taken from the 1st and 3rd platoons, so not too many fellows from my 2nd platoon were injured.

Relative to that article you saw concerning the mistake in bombing, I can easily see how that can happen. All these hills look the same and the fortified positions for our MLR run in a zigzag manner with all kinds of outposts way in front of the line. They have an air attack almost every day and many a time our planes seemingly dive right for us, but always end up hitting a Gook position right in front of ours.

During the time I was on the front lines, only two American planes were shot down. Believe me, if we had Gook planes harassing us all the time like ours harass them, this would be a different type of war.

You asked about frostbite. Outside of the actual casualties inflicted by wounds, we have quite a few fellows that get 1st and 2nd degree frostbite on the fingers. It is not necessarily due to severe cold, because when a firefight (contact with the enemy) occurs, a lot of the guys throw their gloves away so that they can pull the trigger better and the combination of the cold, plus their hands being on the cold steel of their weapons during a long enough period of time, is rough on the hands.

In the platoon-sized raids the Marines always try, with the help of the corpsmen, to bring back all casualties, and KIAS, no matter where or what or how rough the circumstances. Only if a man is killed right out and is in such a position that rescue of the body is impossible (without losing three or four other men in the attempt to get him), will they retreat without a man. If it is a daytime raid, they send out a squad that same night to try to rescue the body before the Gooks drag it off. It is usually during the night raids that we have most of our MIAS (missing in action), because a guy will get wounded or killed in the dark and no one knows what happened to him.

A good buddy of ours, Sidell (that was stationed at Bethesda with us and came over on the 27th draft), got snatched on patrol (along with three other Marines), and is now a prisoner of the Gooks, or worse.

While up on the MLR, we always had all the small arms ammunition we needed (except maybe hand grenades), but from the middle of the month there was always a limit on mortar and artillery ammunition. However, they always reserved enough to hold off a big Gook attack and it hurt the Marines, because they could not put out the usual amount of harassing mortar and artillery fire.

It's funny how a few Marines join the service to come over here and fight, but never leave the states, yet we joined the Navy to stay away from Korea and end up over here. However, I far from regret it. Think of the money I'm saving (ha).

The last couple of days we have had a lot of rain and our tent usually ends up with four ponds on the floor, because it's not the newest tent and is far from leak proof (ha).

Love, Dick

Hi Mom and Dad,   April 6, 1953

I have again sailed the blue Pacific to and from Japan. At one o'clock on the 28th, a Liaison Team with Jerry, myself, and two others from the Medical

Records Office boarded transportation for Ascom City. It's called Tent City because there are rows of tents that house troops in transit to and from their assigned units. We arrived two hours later to pick up our greens (liberty outfits), then headed for K-16, an airstrip near Seoul, Korea.

We couldn't catch a plane for Japan until 2:30 the next morning. Somehow one of the boys in charge lost my travel application card, so I had to wait until the next day to follow the other three on a mail plane leaving for Osaka, Japan. Since we all had our own separate orders, it didn't matter. All we had to do was be in Kobe on the day that the ship (containing the 31st draft) arrived.

Two hours and 15 minutes later, I landed in Japan. By six o'clock that evening I had shaved, changed into my liberty uniform, and converted military scrip into Japanese yen. It takes 360 yen per American dollar.

Well, with my traveling bag and 23,000 yen in my pocket, I left the air base gate and called for a rickshaw to take me the short distance to the train station. It took ⅑th of a dollar or 40 yen to go about 10 miles to Osaka, the second largest city in Japan, next to Tokyo. Since very few service men are stationed near Osaka, very few people speak English. What a time!

That night in Osaka, I checked into the Naniwa Hotel and then went out to see a little of the city. A taxi only costs 80 to 150 yen and will take you almost anywhere in the city. They all drive like madmen and would be completely lost without their horns, which they blow continuously. The Japanese people are fascinating and friendly. I spent two hours in one shop trying to get the people to understand me relative to buying a beautiful sewing machine. They had three translating dictionaries, plus five guys that could speak a little English, in the deal before we got done. Could have bought it, had it packed, insured, and delivered to Ohio for $85, but didn't. Trying to bargain prices when you can't speak Japanese is quite a trick.

That night it only took an hour to get to Kobe. You can buy a swell meal for 300 to 500 yen in any of the better chop-chop houses. For four days it was the life of Riley staying in the oriental-style hotel, traveling by taxi, shaving by Jap barbers, eating in chop-chop restaurants. A few gifts will be coming home for you by mail. Between taking pictures, shopping, sightseeing and the like, those four days passed quickly. We were completely on our own and did what we wanted to, when we wanted to. Really great liberty!

Boy, it didn't take long for the Japanese people to get the word that the ship with the 31st draft of Marines was coming in. The prices really jumped that night! The city turned into a booming metropolis and really went after the American dollar. We had a great advantage that night, because we knew what most of the prices should be and could speak enough Jap language by then, so that they couldn't pull the wool over our eyes.

Once we got on the ship and went to work on the health records, it only took one and a half days to complete them. We had great bunks and quarters on the transport ship coming back, usually sleeping in until 8:00.

We pulled into the Inchon Harbor at 10 and were on the 1st boat to go ashore. After a couple of hours in Seoul, we got back at H. and S. Company by 5:00 chowtime. Really a smooth and wonderful week's vacation. When we got back, we had five packages and four letters from you, plus quite a few other letters.

We also learned that our old outfit 2/5 had been hit hard. They had just gone back into reserve and the 1st and 3rd Battalions were on line when the Gooks hit the Marine lines. Maybe you saw articles on "Vegas," "Carson" and a few other outposts getting hit. Also "Old Baldy" which is just to the right of our outfit and held by the Army. The total battle took more than four days and nights and I still don't know the correct number of KIAS and casualties. Over 20 corpsmen within our own Battalion were wounded and I understand three were killed. That doesn't include the 67 Marines killed and 760 Marine casualties. We were in Japan while all this was happening and so we don't know the exact figures. Our present Battalion went up to help and had many casualties so you can imagine how many the other outfits had. A couple of companies were almost completely wiped out.

Some of the stories I heard were really gory. Maybe someday I will get the straight scoop. If this had happened two months ago, we would have been in the middle of it. I remember one little corpsmen that came into BAS just three days before we left for the rear. Well, they say he was killed during the ordeal. All I can say is, I bet Knowles, and a couple of other corpsmen we still knew out at 2/5 (who hadn't been rotated yet), were sure jumping. Most of them had to go back up on the lines.

Love, Dick

Dear Ma and Pa,   April 11, 1953

The morning we pulled into Tokyo it poured down rain, but then was good weather thereafter. From the air the Japan fields look like a quilt, all in squares, with brown rice paddies next to small green fields.

By the time we traveled by trolley to Tokyo, and got some Japanese yen and a good meal, it was afternoon. That evening I stayed in a swanky Hotel. The next day I wanted to do some sightseeing, but thought I had better start for Kobe in case the ship we were sent over to meet came early. On the full 11 hour ride I got to see much of the country (as beautiful as California, with similar climate and orange trees) and didn't seem too tired when I got to Kobe. Their soft, well-irrigated land limits the use of any big [farming] equipment.

I met several friendly Japanese men on the train who could speak English. One even wanted me to stop and attend his friend's wedding (ha ha). By eight that evening I arrived in Kobe and went to stay in the New Kobe Hotel where Fries (the First Class [petty officer] in charge of us) said he would stay. He didn't, and I didn't like the hotel, so the next morning, when I found Dick, we moved to a very oriental hotel for the remainder of our time in Kobe. It was up on a mountainside, away from the city and strictly Japanese style, with many civilians staying there. You have to take your shoes off when entering and they warm the rooms with heated charcoal. We talked mostly to a Japanese lady manager who called herself Mitzie and was a lot of fun. She could understand English fairly well and had our clothes pressed, our bath water prepared, and our chow ordered. Since an old *papa-san,* the doorman, was trying to learn English, and us Japanese, we all had a lot of fun. I had several Jap baths in the big tubs, almost like going swimming. The water, as hot as you can stand it, was almost too hot for me.

The hotel was all on one floor spread out over a large area with small gardens in the middle. All the hotel doors were sliding, panel type, and with coal-heated rooms it paid to keep them closed. As you can see we are wearing Kimonos in some of the pictures Dick took.

I was so occupied with looking around and shopping in Kobe, Japan, that I seldom bought more than one good meal per day, and, for a buck and a half, I could buy a full course dinner. I found several nice places to go dancing and spent a lot of my time there. All the girls can sing the American songs and dance well.

The last ten days have gone by like a flash and now I'm back at Able Medical Hospital. It was almost a sure thing that the 22nd draft would go home with the 21st draft, until the 5th Marines got hit, including many corpsmen. The last couple of nights the 7th have been getting hit up on "Carson."

It was sure good to get all those boxes when we got back from Japan. The cans nicely protect the cookies.

Love, Jerry

Hi Mom and Dad,   April 16, 1953

I've sent home pictures I took of Kobe, Japan, including a back alley near Kobe Kanko Hotel, a statue of an elephant in the hotel's driveway, the little garden just outside our room, a family on the street, a little girl with a baby on her back, and some children playing.

I've figured up how much work I've done on the Mimeograph machine the last 42 days and it totaled 86,000 copies of paper.

Jerry in the garden area of the hotel in Kobe, Japan

So Kenny Lohr is another one on the list for marriage plans, hey! When we figured what's happening to the fellows we used to run around with, we came up with: Kenny Kline and Virgil Marsh (Air Force Flyboys), Russell Tisher (Army Doggie), Dixie Baird (Navy Swabbie), Ronnie Newcome (Hooked), Frank Leonard (Civilian College Student), Skip Maur (College Student), Kenny Lohr (Marriage Plans), Don Myers (Marriage Plans), Bruce Patterson (Senior in High School), and Jim Hudson (there's one boy that jumps around so much from school to work, or both, that at the present I'm not sure where or what he is doing). Jack Chin is still running loose. About the only girls in our class that aren't married are Pat Raush, Doris Porter, Maxine Skilton, Mary Wiles, and Dorothy Bowen. So Skippy Koba has a new car, hey! Must be pulling in a big check.

Love, Dick

Hi Mom and Dad,   April 29, 1953

"Happy Birthday Mother" and "Happy Wedding Anniversary Parents" from your loving sons. Here are some hints about the gifts you will be receiving. We are glad that you finally received some of our gifts. Were the robes torn or ripped in any manner? How about the magazines, were they torn into threads?

Well, April 21st started the exchange of prisoners. Three corpsmen from our office went up to the British section of line to represent the division and they said that the condition of the prisoners was good. First the prisoners are exchanged at Panmunjom and then are taken by ambulance to "Freedom Village." Our corpsmen said they seemed to be fairly well fed and, although they had not been given the excellent medical care that our doctors could have given them, they had been treated by doctors. The prisoners said that the Chinese Communists more or less left them to themselves, as long as they gave the Commies no trouble. Most of them were flabbergasted and could hardly believe that they were once again free men. Apparently they even had several types of recreation, because some had something broken because of a sport they were playing.

You may remember me telling about a boy named Sidell that I knew back at Bethesda who had been snatched by the Gooks some time back. Well, he came back in the prisoner exchange deal and I was sure glad to hear it.

Knowles, a good friend of ours, was the last of the boys from BAS 2/5 that we knew. He was relieved a few days ago and claims that they really worked up a sweat for about five days when the 5th Regiment was getting hit. I believe him!

My partner (a marine named Hackett) and I were the 6th team to be eliminated in an eight team horseshoe pitching tournament that lasted four days.

I don't believe we've ever received a box with mold in it. If we did, we ate it mold and all (ha).

Well, that is it for today.

Love, Dick

Dear Ma and Pa,   May 22, 1953

Good to hear that the vases came through in one piece. Must have been worth the couple extra 100 yen for the packing job. Ethel Hill's letter mentioned that Larry has been swimming down at Jim Hudson's swimming hole already.

The Marines have finally gone into Corps Reserve after refusing it several times, I guess because they took a real beating and could use the rest. H. and S. Company will stay right here.

I am surprised at the vegetation over here. All the bushes grow on the hillsides and what few trees there are blossom out and cover up the ground, giving this place a good look. Some mosquitoes are showing up. We have been lucky to have been in Korea during months when there were none around. The main complaint over here is the dust. That's why I haven't gone to Seoul, because a trip on the roads usually gets a guy good and dirty. Even after a big rain the dust is back in a day or so.

We had an overgrown pup as our tent mascot that one of the Marines took care of. All of a sudden it just died and we didn't know why. Everyone

Corpsman Knowles at the battalion aid station

thought it might be poison, because it couldn't seem to breathe. Some doctor came up with the answer: it was a form of distemper with pneumonia, causing a blue liquid in the lungs that suddenly becomes active and usually suffocates the animal. There are three dogs on the compound, all friendly. One is a big collie-chow combination that makes a good watchdog, helping us make our rounds during our fire watch. The Koreans eat their dogs, so four guys that work here think a lot of the ones we have. The dogs seem to know it, because they won't let the Korean workers near them. Speaking of dogs, how are our Laddie and Blackie getting along? They probably are wondering where we have been for the last nine months.

I've been going to church services. We got a new Chaplain who seems like a good chap. Loud, but interesting and he puts some good points across. The Chaplains over here do a good job, especially the ones assigned to the regiments. When we were on line, they came up and held services right out in the open.

Well what do you know, we got five new guys in the office and just about everybody has an assistant now. Mine helps me on the Health Record desk and will probably take over the job when it is time for me to be rotated home.

One of the Sergeants in our office had to go home on emergency leave due to his mother being sick with only a month to live. Everybody chipped into a donation of about $120 bucks to help pay for some of his expenses. He was glad to see the money. That's the latest.

Love, Jerry

Hi Mom and Dad, June 17, 1953

So I only lack $25 dollars from having $2000 in the bank, that's great!!

We got the razor and Kool Aid along with the big box of marshmallows, chocolates, dates and cookies. Thanks a million!

The 33rd draft of Marines and Corpsmen arrived about the 5th of June and the 23rd draft returned on the ship. If all goes according to plan, the 24th draft goes back in July and the 25th in August. MacGowan, a corpsman from our old Battalion who lives in Akron and is among the 23rd draft, said he would give you a call for us when he gets home.

Last week, I had a private jeep driver and jeep and went all over our area collecting personal material from fellows in the different Med Companies. Snapped three rolls of film while driving around the country.

Dad, if our old Plymouth is still hitting on all cylinders, then we will do most of our driving in it, however, on certain occasions (hint) we would appreciate the use of the Buick.

Wow, five cans of milk. That's more than we ever used to get. The cows must really be shelling out. We would like to be home on leave in July, but the Marines don't figure it that way. I would just as soon be throwing bales around as some of the things I have been doing around here lately, like clearing the weeds around the medical records section.

Oh, our latest USO show was none other than Dick Contino and his band. It was really good. The weather changes from hot and humid to the opposite, dreary, rainy, and damp. Ronnie's latest letter says he's to be married to Virginia one hour ahead of Bob Folger and Margie on the 14th of June. Kenny Kline wrote to us after our return and said we could have called him from anywhere in Japan, free of charge, if we would have known about it.

Thanks again for sending our electric razor and some Kool Aid.

Love, Dick

Dear Ma and Pa, June 23, 1953

We had some excitement around the 1st of June. The whole sky lit up with flares and Able Med was given the word to get ready to either evacuate all of their patients or prepare for a bunch of new casualties. The Army lost several outposts and somebody pushed the panic button and started the word that the Gooks had broken through the MLR and were headed for Seoul. The 1st Marines were called back up to the Kansas line as a support unit. The Turks [Turkey contributed an infantry brigade to the UN forces in Korea] replaced our troops in a couple of sections and they are considered the roughest outfit in Korea. They were hit by *taka-san* Gooks and did a good job of holding.

Morin and I went from Medical Records to Freedom Village to set up and have a dress rehearsal for the Big Prisoner Switch. We will be working with two doctors in receiving, where we will have to be sure all wounds are covered with bandages so they can be dusted with a powder that kills all bugs or lice they may have picked up as prisoners. Freedom Village consists of five long tents for the receiving, dusting, and treatment of POWs (prisoners of war). We will be working in the tent for the Commonwealth (English, New Zealanders, etc.). Since the communists were supposed to send us the more badly wounded last time, we aren't expecting many in bad shape this time. The Army will have its 45th MASH Hospital set up to treat serious cases and copter them out. Rumors are that there will be a total of 12,000 POWs, giving us about 2000 of them. Could be fun.

You wouldn't think there was going to be peace the way we hear sirens lately, the first one usually coming about the middle of the movie, which means all lights go out including the movie projector.

One of the sergeants in our tent bought a new puppy for 3½ cartons of cigarettes, so once again we have a mascot. He's a beaut, contented, has *taka-san* hair, is not too big, and is about half house-broken. Does his dirty work outside.

Got a letter from the Kent Aunts [Frances and Louise Hoskins], the Freedom grandparents [Charlie and Gladys Chappell], and Frank Leonard. Frank gave us the lowdown on his latest activities and claims that Frank Jones and George Burketh are both out of the service now. Aunt Francis sent a couple of pictures of her which we will add to our pinups. Have written to and talked to Bobby Day on the phone a few times and swapped rotation rumors. He said Beck has had quite a tour of the Mediterranean countries and got to pull a lot of liberties. Have you seen a movie called "Battle Circus" about corpsmen and the Medical Corps?

Albertson and Bloxsom came down for some card games. We have a bet with them for going home on the ship—whoever wins the most card games will have to be treated to all of the ice cream (sundaes, sodas, milkshakes, etc.) they can eat when we hit Frisco. They are both in on the Big Switch and have to be on one-hour alert, so they were told to move into Able Medical Company in case something should come up all of a sudden.

Love, Jerry

Dear Ma and Pa,   July 8, 1953

Well the Marines are back in the news and it doesn't take long for them to get things stirred up. They went back up on the line and by the way the casualties are coming into Able Med it looks like they jumped-off to try to take back the Berlin outposts, or they were overrun. I've already heard that one company was wiped out except for three men.

Now for the good news. Mr. Cottini [Officer in charge] put our names in for R and R in Japan and Dick and I are taking off for the R and R center in Kyoto. Should have much more time to do things this time. It will be our last time to see the Orient and so we are taking advantage of it. Will do a lot of picture taking, not spend too much money, but still have a good time.

I've been losing my excess weight and now weigh about 165 pounds.

Love, Jerry

Hi Mom and Dad,   July 16, 1953

We are back again following a wonderful trip! We left here July 9th, spent the night in Ascom City, and caught a plane at the airbase. By 1:00 we were on a bus leaving Itami airbase in Japan. By 2:30 we were at Camp Fisher where we were issued two clean and freshly pressed sets of khaki liberty clothes along with a steak dinner. And shortly after a shower, we found ourselves on a 4½ day vacation in oriental Japan.

The special R and R Hotel in Kyoto, Japan, offers rooms for three dollars a night and three meals a day for a dollar. Each table has its own cute Jap girl who brings whatever you order right out and immediately takes the plate away as soon as you suggest you are through eating. If you want a cigarette, she's right there with a light. Order ice tea, and she brings three glasses for each person.

At 7:30 the 2nd morning, after a filling breakfast, we hopped on an electric train with John Gass, a friend from 2/5, and headed for Japan's second largest city, Osaka. We saw the city, took in the famous castle, snapped pictures, and, at night, rented a row boat for a couple of hours to see parts of the city from the river that runs through it. It is beautiful because of the little lighted lanterns shining down from the city and from other boats.

The next day we visited Nara, once the capital of Japan, and its many points of interest (all wooden temples, buddhas, etc.). We hired three rickshaws pulled by middle-aged *papa-sans* (paid them $2.50 for the afternoon). Everyplace we went, the little bit of Japanese language we knew sure came in handy. We also used the trolley systems which you can travel on for hours for only 10 yen (around 4 cents). That night we returned to the R and R Hotel in Kyoto, then shopped the narrow streets from six to 10 when all the businesses are lit up. Cars are not driven on many of the store-lined streets.

The last day we guided John on a shopping spree and then toured Kyoto's pottery factory where they make the most beautiful vases, and other dishes, that I have ever seen.

The trip cost around $200 bucks, including gifts.

Love, Dick and Jerry

Hi Mom and Dad,   July 28, 1953

They are talking Big Switch again. Wish it would have gone through when I was in on it. The 7th Marines have taken a lot of casualties in the last couple of weeks. I heard there were 28 wounded, six dead, and three missing in action for the corpsmen in one regiment alone.

The Marines are definitely back on the line catching the headlines. The 7th Regiment is almost nil after losing Berlin and East Berlin in one of the bloodiest battles of the war. Baker Med has been working day and night just taking care of casualties and Able has been jumping too. For a couple of days around here there were so many copters flying in that one couldn't get out of sight until the next showed up. If I know those Marines, they will try to take the outposts back and that means gobs more casualties. The bulk of the communist Gook attacks hit and took the same outposts (East Berlin and Berlin) my old outfit maintained forward of where we spent our time with the 2 Bn/5 Reg Aid Station.

Well, wait a big minute! The word now is that in about 30 minutes they are going to sign an armistice. We, the Marines, whom we have been with for one year and 14 days now, hope this transaction takes place.

Glad to hear that Grandpa is improving fast and that the hay hauling came off successfully. Bob Folger looks like he is getting thin in the wedding picture you forwarded. I am going down to Division to mail a box home full of green wool pants and hope it doesn't collect mildew.

Hurray!! We just got the word that the Armistice was signed, today, July 27th. That's just great! All firing must stop 12 hours later. Well that's enough good news for one day from this short timer.

Love, Dick

Dear Ma and Pa,   August 7, 1953

We were packed, checked out of the Medical Battalion, and headed for Ascom City on the 2nd of August. Our disembarkation date, for boarding the USNS *Walker*, has been set back five days. On each day of the 4th, 5th, and 6th, they told us we were going to leave the next day. Maybe we will make it around noon today the 7th.

We are going to be the last draft to head for the states for several months, I guess because our ship was already on the way to pick us up. The 25th and 26th drafters are really mad.

Here at Ascom City they've had movies every night for us, but I had seen them all. We have spent most of our five days here playing Pinochle. Albertson and Bloxsom are already five games ahead of us, but there is a long trip coming up. It's been raining hard, so one day we had a river running right through our tent. Had to wash a pair of dungarees for the first time, will sure miss the *mama-san* method of laundry service. Expect 13 or 14 days for the trip back.

                                                          Love, Jerry

Hi Mom and Dad,   August 12, 1953

Well tonight I'll start off by saying it's a beautiful night and at the present time I am where I can observe it. The air is still, with just a slight breeze and with our shirts off we are comfortable. I am sitting out on the main deck of the troop ship the USNS *Walker*. We can see the city lights of Inchon and the three Navy Hospital ships (*Laudia, Repose,* and *Haven*) around us in the harbor.

At dark, three nights ago, we boarded the *Walker* and now it is three days later. We have just been sitting out here in the harbor waiting for a group of "Returnees" (prisoners of war that will go back to the states with us). Tonight, about six o'clock, we got 175 of them. How many more we will get, and how many more days until we head for home, we don't know.

We have heard that because we are using up a portion of our food supply, we will probably go to Japan to stock up a supply large enough to last for our trip. That means a couple more days. When the POWs boarded ship they all had on new Army clothes and looked fairly good. They have been processed and reprocessed since their return to our lines. By now you folks in the states have probably been hearing all kinds of stories about them.

We have been getting three good meals a day and haven't had to stand in very long lines like we did coming over. In the first place there are less troops now compared to our trip over and the ship is larger. The

Prisoners of war on stretchers after loading onto the deck of the USNS *Walker*

weather is better and we aren't all crowded together. It's a much nicer ship in all respects.

On the end of the ship, right on deck, they show the movies and it's really nice. Then on the other end of the ship, on deck, they have large flood lights by which you can see to write letters or play cards. The sleeping compartments are rather stuffy even though a ventilation system is working at all times. However, I haven't found it difficult to sleep yet.

There is only one gripe that the fellows have. All the showers are salt water and, until you take a salt water shower, you wouldn't know what I mean. Unless you use a special type of soap, a lather is almost impossible and you come out feeling sticky all over.

We got to see the new draft (35th) of Marines come in, including 160 corpsmen, who will have to spend 14 months over here. Poor guys!

This will probably be my last letter until I'm back stateside, and I still can't guess when we will hit California. However, be watching the papers because, with these prisoners of war aboard and this being the first ship to return following the armistice, the write up may be a little larger.

Love, Dick

Reflections

JERRY: While Dick and I were busy coping with flooded tents and playing the role of "record keepers" in the Able Medical complex (the Bethesda of the Orient), some of our peer corpsmen (such as Bill Brocker and Swede Anderson) were assigned to MASH-like surgical units. Their stories of their difficult days were never pleasant. Heavy nights would begin with minor cases, making the surgical crew think only a small group had been hit; then the place would fill up. It was a matter of operating, finishing, going out to the pre-op ward, picking another case, having the litter bearers bring him in, working one after another on a neck injury, a leg, a belly. The wounded would lie there, muttering stories of comrades falling on grenades to save a platoon. Many had broken bones and chests full of blood. Some of them lived; many of them didn't. Because of their protective flak jackets, they generally had wounds of the extremities and bruises of the chest, back, and abdomen, where a fragment of shell had hit the jacket but did not penetrate. They were young men, all reacting differently to their injuries and pain. Some, having had morphine, would lie quietly, thinking or sleeping. Others would moan and cry out for hours.

I often wondered if Dick and I could have been more useful in helping with the surgical treatment of the wounded in the field hospital setting. Sure, keeping medical records straight, especially in my job as Division Health Locator, was an important contribution, and to my knowledge I did a yeomen's job. Also, as an aside, my understanding is that thousands of such military health records were lost at the end of the Vietnam War.

DICK: During both of our trips to Japan (the first for duty handling the records of an incoming marine draft ship, the second for rest and recuperation) we escaped enemy attacks of major significance. The Second Battalion of the Fifth Marines, to which we had been assigned only months earlier, took a beating on both occasions. As we arrived back at Able Medical Hospital after each Japan trip, we learned that had we still been on the front line or in a BAS with those troops, we could well have lost our lives.

Chapter Eight

Military Sea Transportation Service

$\mathcal{T}$he letters of this chapter report the final adventure of our tour of duty in the military service: our transportation of refugees out of North Vietnam. In September 1953, prior to that assignment, we returned to the United States for an uneventful year of duty in the dispensary at Camp Pendleton, California. The joys of that year were the marvelous weekend liberties in Los Angeles and Hollywood. We attended many USO dances, sports events (especially football games—on Saturday UCLA, and on Sunday the Los Angeles Rams), and movies, and we learned to ski in the mountains.

We saw over thirty excellent plays, including *Brigadoon, Dial M for Murder, Stalag 17, The Lady's Not for Burning, The Seven Year Itch,* and *Porgy and Bess.*

Perhaps to have had all those wonderful postwar fun and games was some kind of reward for having endured and survived a year in Korea. One thing was for sure, the cities of Los Angeles and Hollywood were good to servicemen like us. They handed out all kinds of tickets to anyone in uniform.

Or perhaps those good times were a kind of prepayment for our last big assignment in the service. While we were having fun in California, President Eisenhower promised South Vietnam's prime minister, Ngo Dinh Diem, that the United States would help his government develop and maintain a strong, viable state capable of resisting subversion or armed aggression. In support of Diem, the United States poured $250 million per year into South Vietnam.

The most important happening of the Diem period was the dramatic story of the flight of 880,000 Catholic refugees to the South. The refugees consisted of two groups. The first was the more than a hundred thousand Vietnamese troops of the colonial army, and their dependents. These men, who had fought many years against the Viet Minh, were fearful of staying in North Vietnam. The second group was about six hundred thousand Vietnamese Catholics. Diem terrified those people by telling them the communists would prohibit all their religious services and symbols and put their priests on trial. Led by confused parish priests, manipulated by their own leaders and their bureaucratic allies in the cities, the Catholics began their flight south to South Vietnam. Units of the U.S. Seventh Fleet, including our Military Sea Transport ship, the USNS *Marine Lynx,* played the key role in moving the refugees, and the U.S. government provided ninety-three million dollars for their resettlement. Since they were anticommunists and uncompromising in their opposition to the Viet Minh, Diem incorporated these Catholics into his political base, appointing many of them to top posts in his administration.

Letters

Dear Ma and Pa,   August 26, 1954

The first day back to work following the Labor Day LA [Los Angeles] weekend, we received our new orders requesting that we report to Fort Mason, San Francisco, California on 9-9-54. Being that Red Reynolds and Jerry Ross both received orders also, it worked out swell for us to ride up with them (which also made it handy for us to haul our gear).

Looks like we are not going to have a dull remaining six months in the service. We fly from Moffett Field (Naval Air Station) to Saigon, Indo-China, where we will meet our new ship (a sea going sailor at last—ha). Forty-five of us corpsmen (which includes a mess of guys we know, like Dick Holt) are to meet three MSTS ships (Military Sea Transportation Service) in Saigon Harbor and then proceed to evacuate non-communist civilians out of North Indo-China. Our next mailing address will be Military Department, USNS *Marine Lynx* (T-AP 194) c/o F.P.O. San Francisco, California.

It sounds like wonderful duty and a good chance to see a little more of the world. We are now back in the Navy again, but still have to wear Marine clothes. Hope our Navy outfits catch up with us in the next six months. Today we both sent boxes home containing Marine Corps gear. Please check it over closely when you take it apart to prevent any of our cockroaches from making a new home in Ravenna. Ha.

Love, Jerry

Hi Mom and Dad, September 14, 1954

We received liberty in San Francisco from Friday to Monday, and, because they had no place to keep us on the base, they paid us ($9 a day) to live in town. Not bad hey? All three nights we went dancing at the USOs, met some very nice girls and had a splendid weekend. We rode the famous cable car, visited the popular Fisherman's Wharf, and stayed in the El Cortez Hotel.

This afternoon we boarded a bus, bag and baggage, and came out to Moffett Field. We will stay here tonight and then fly out at 10:00 in the morning. Nine of us are going to the *Lynx*, including Ross and Reynolds, so you might say we are taking our own crew.

Love, Dick

Dear Ma and Pa, September 19, 1954

Saturday we arrived aboard the USS *Cavallaro* [High speed transport ship] which is docked right off of one of the main streets on a river in Saigon. The trip for its distance was one of the best I have ever been on. Our total time in the air was about 35 hours. Before leaving the States, Dick and I pulled Monday night liberty in San Jose which is just a short distance from Moffett Naval Air Station. Our first stop on the flight was a good one at Barber's Point, Hawaii. We were too tired (after a 10 hour flight) to make a trip into Honolulu, so we went over to the dispensary where we saw four guys that we knew. One of them was Stellwag (the Long Island Corps School buddy who took us up to his home for a weekend). He claims he is going to go to Mount Union College in Alliance, Ohio, so we gave him our home address and told him to look us up about April. From Barber's Point it was a straight through trip (9 hours) with breather stops at an island called Kwajalein, then on to Guam (6½ hours) and the air station of Sangley Point near Manila in the Philippines. We had box lunches on the plane and perfect flying conditions.

Being that we flew over southern Indo-China during the day-light hours, it gave us a splendid opportunity to view the country and general lay-of-the-land. Indo-China has a lot of vegetation and swamp area that surrounds huge rivers with many distributing branches. Actually, much of the transportation is by way of water canals that intermingle between the cities and farmland. When we got to Saigon's only air station (which is French), we were taken through the city on a bus right to the river where we loaded a flag ship to wait the arrival of our own ship. The uss *Cavallaro* is a hot, small boat and rather crowded.

Saigon surprised me. I expected to see another Inchon or Seoul. The city has some fine looking modern buildings. Most of the Indo-Chinese men wear short pants, including the French, to keep cool. The women wear long, silky pants. The Rickshaw and bicycle are the main methods of transportation downtown. Their money is the *piastre* and equals about 60 per one American dollar.

We went on liberty from about one to nine yesterday and did a lot of walking around and looking. Had a big steak dinner at a recommended hotel and it didn't go down too well. Today we will probably get out and take some pictures. It seems funny to spend one weekend in Frisco and the next in Saigon, about 8000 miles away. Just goes to show you they get around in the Navy. Ha. Our ship is scheduled to pull in here next Tuesday.

Well hope everything is going okay at home and that you get this right away. Who knows, maybe we will end up with an Indo-China album to add to our collection.

Love, Jerry

Hi Mom and Dad,   September 19, 1954

I am really surprised and greatly impressed by the city of Saigon. They have a collection of intermingled people and races over here like I have never seen before (Indians, Chinese, French, etc). The city is quite modern, mostly due to the progress that has been contributed from the French. Saigon is located inland a number of miles up a huge river [the Saigon River] (not a port city).

The job of our ship (the *Marine Lynx*) is to travel north a couple hundred more miles and pick up Chinese refugees and then bring them back down here to Saigon. Everything around here is on a "truce" basis and these refugees have a choice of remaining communists in their homeland or becoming non-communists down here at Saigon (Nationalist Indo-China).

Actually, although things are quite peaceful around here now, about six weeks ago they were engaged in a war. The weather is very tropical because we are close to the equator. Rain comes and goes. The first couple of days it took us a while to adjust to the heat. Very few people speak English and a lot of them speak French. However, that doesn't do us much good. I knew I should have taken French in high school. Ha. They have several very fine French Hotels, restaurants, and quite a few modern department stores.

As always.

Love, Dick

Hi Mom and Dad,   September 24, 1954

Parlez-vous Français? That means, do you speak French? I have been studying a little French during our four-day trip up along the Indo-China coast. We boarded our ship, the *Marine Lynx,* as scheduled on the 21st. During the last four days we have been adapting ourselves to the daily procedures and routine aboard the ship. In the first place we were not expected by the regular crew, so therefore find that we are extra help rather than badly needed help.

There are around 100,000 refugees who have chosen to move down into the southern section or Nationalist Indo-China. Our job will last only as long as the refugees do. We boarded the ship following the unloading of a load of them. Therefore we received our first taste of what working with them is going to be like.

Believe me, the smell of their quarters was just like a barnyard which hadn't been cleaned in the last year. From some of the tales the regular corpsmen related to us, I look for the next trip down the coast to be very interesting.

The complete trip from Saigon (a Southern sector city) to some city in the Northern sector takes about 10 days. Of the 10 days, we have the Chinese aboard four of them. The other six days we do very little work.

Our quarters are separated from all the other quarters on the ship and I must admit they are truly the nicest ones aboard. Not only are they clean, but also air-conditioned. The chow is wonderful (even better than at Staff Quarters at Camp Pendleton) and a pleasant colored boy serves us in the fashionable style of restaurant waiter. Since there are less than 40 military personnel aboard, we are treated in the best of style. All the other crewmen are civilians. Incidentally, this ship is just like the *Marine Serpent* that we went to Korea on.

I am hurrying this letter off, because the mail ship meets ours only every five days. We just got your letter saying that Dad has been sick in bed for over two weeks. Since it's rare for him to be sick for longer than three days, we are hoping it isn't anything serious.

As for our Navy clothes, well I just hope that some day (before we get discharged) they catch up with us. Hope you sent them in a seabag. To top everything off, they don't even wear Blues here because of the hot weather. Neither the Doctor nor the Chief mind that we are still wearing Marine clothes.

Most of today we spent wrapping gift packages for the refugees (about 2000). Each package consists of two pounds of rice, a pack of American cigarettes, and a slip of paper with Chinese writing on it (probably welcoming them aboard).

Yesterday we received four shots including Typhus, Cholera, Typhoid, and Plague. Naturally our arms are a bit sore. Ha.

Well I have rattled on long enough, so I shall sign off for today.

Au revoir (good bye), *ce soir* (this evening).

Love, Dick

Dear Ma and Pa,   September 26 and 28, 1954

Tues morning we left Saigon and traveled for several days up to a bay of uncertain name, which we will call Touraine Bay. It is just south of the 17th parallel and the most northern possession of the Chinese Nationalists. There we sat and picked up some mail and new movies. From there we came on up to our present location, which is among a group of islands out in the Haiphong [North Vietnam] Harbor. Soon we will take on a load of civilians and hi-ball it for Saigon before the ship starts to smell too much.

We've been going out to local beaches, where the sand is plentiful, and have had a fine time swimming in tropical waters and lounging on sandy beaches under palm trees. It is easy to swim and float in the clean ocean salt water. Red has a diving mask that we use to look at the coral rock on the bottom of a shallow area. We will be here in this area for several days.

So far my main duty has been office work. Most of the movies on board are old ones that I have seen. I am anxious to see if the Cleveland Indians win the series. We get very little news at our present location. I'm reading "Kings Row" at present.

Love, Jerry

Dear Mom and Dad,   September 29, 1954

Our ship (plus about 10 others) has been sitting out here in the bay for the last 10 days.

During the last week we have been living the life of pleasure with trips to the beach every day. The ship sends a small lifeboat out to an island beach twice a day (at noon and at four). This is rather weird country up here but still very interesting and picturesque. Hundreds of little islands all tower high above the bay as huge rock cliffs. Intermingled between and on the sides of the rock islands are small, sandy beaches. The water is warm, clear, and very salty. All the islands have plant and vegetable life and many of them also have baboons. Most of the guys have been collecting beautiful shells. Its been an enjoyable way to pass the time. With my trusty camera I have been able to get some pictures of the beaches and of Saigon.

We should be picking up our load today or tomorrow.

Love, Dick

Jerry admiring the view at the top of an island off the coast of Vietnam

Dear Ma and Pa,   October 7, 1954

All in all this trip turned out to be much better than what we heard about the last one. The people that we carried were in far better shape and very few of them were sick or in bad shape physically. On Sunday the 3rd we loaded 2500 of them by means of small French ships that brought them out to meet the ship from a nearby city. What it amounted to was a load of troops and their families. These people came from a city just north of the Vietnam border (the [region of] Red China country on the other side). Most of them spoke Chinese, which did not help when it came time to treat them [because] most of the interpreters spoke Vietnamese.

Each family ranged from five members on up and when they came they brought all of their valuables with them that they could possibly carry. Everybody that could walk carried something. Even the old women were carrying loads that we would not [have wanted] to carry very far. Just about all the females (that are old enough to have a baby) were carrying babies. It seems like it takes these people a long time to grow up (so that they don't look to be under fifteen) and once they have passed that stage, they look ancient. Anyway they manage to carry everything but the chickens and the outhouse.

Luckily the entire trip back to Saigon was very smooth and we didn't have to worry about the people getting seasick which always presents a very messy problem. All of the crew, including us, have to help with the loading. The main trouble in loading the people is getting them all a bunk and getting them to stay in it until everyone has one. One compartment will be almost full with only seven racks left to fill and then a family of eight will come next in line and it is impossible to separate them. They will also leave the upper bunks empty and take the lower ones so that later the upper ones are spread out all over [but still] the families will not split up and find themselves empty bunks. It takes almost a day to load 2500 with all of the complications.

The first evening after the load was loaded, we went around for a sick call to try and find seriously ill passengers. Six were admitted to our ward, including two babies that were as thin as toothpicks from malnutrition. On the last day of the trip one of them died. And at the last minute we had a birth. We heard that on the last trip two died down in the compartments before the corpsmen even knew they were sick.

The people are comical in some ways. They use the drinking fountains for washing their clothes and bathing the babies. They also use the commodes for everything from their proper use to washing the family's clothes, bathing the babies, and shaving. Of course the little kids have been brought up to urinate on the local street and they don't change over night in the compartments. Each day the smell of the people is much more noticeable. We have to change clothes and take a shower after each sick call we hold in the compartments. The sickbay (with the exception of the people that come to sickcall) is not patronized by the passengers so we escape the smell most of the time. We will have to go someplace to have the compartments fumigated before the ship can carry American passengers again.

We had a midwife and nurse on board to help take care of the Vietnamese patients. The midwife was about 25 and cute, but neither one could speak a word of English so we couldn't sit around and chat for very long. The few interpreters aboard were worth their weight in gold, but it seemed like every time we needed one they couldn't be found.

Love, Jerry

Dear Mom and Dad,   October 7, 1954

Yesterday we pulled into Saigon, unloaded the 2500 refugees, and finished my first trip (three days with the people).

When we first loaded all of them, we helped direct traffic, assisted in carrying the heavier personal gear aboard, and instructed them in use of such ship utilities as the drinking fountain. All the daily instruments and objects of common use to us tended to puzzle them and so we had to explain.

The civilian crew members had the biggest job upon their shoulders in that they had to make the refugees clean up the compartments. From past habit and up-bringing most of them lacked the knowledge of our sanitation methods of waste disposal and cleanliness.

Everybody from little junior to old grandma carry a bundle of gear that generally weighs more than they do. Most of our cases of illness are little babies who look like they are still wearing the clothes they were given at birth. To make the task of the crewmen difficult, they eat their chow right on the floor and have the tendency to keep all left over food (the combination of rice and fish) which creates an odor very disagreeable to our American nostrils.

Through great effort on the crewmen's part, plus illustrative examples of how to sweep and swab the floors, they finally learned how to clean up the compartments.

Each day at 8 and 2 o'clock four teams of us corpsmen (consisting of two men within a team) made the rounds of the compartments in search of sick refugees. We carried with us small first aid kits (about the size of those we used in Korea) that contained six basic medicines, namely aspirin for head-aches, Dramamine for sea sickness, Chloroquine for fever, Merthiolate for body sores, and Bacitracin ointment for eyes with puss.

It was impossible to give each and everyone that was sick the private atten-tion of a doctor, because for such a task it would take a hundred doctors and two tons of medicine. Therefore we proceeded to treat, as best we could, all the minor illnesses and separated those requiring the attention of a doctor. During our rounds of the first sick call we had to search and examine every child for the mothers were afraid that we might hurt them in some manner. Also they seemed to believe that, if they once became separated from their family, they would never find them again. By not understanding our lan-guage, plus having heard negative propaganda about us, they were very cau-tious. With those two common fears, they at first strongly hesitated to bring our attention to body sores, high fevers, or any other illness of their children. However, as the trip progressed and we made our helpful and friendly pur-pose known, their tone soon changed to the point where the mothers were more than happy to point out everything wrong with their kids. Ha.

In the case of the more severely ill, it is rather difficult for the doctors to determine the definite cause, because the child may have three different diseases. It is really amazing, in my opinion, that any of these people live to be 25. Its hard to determine age, for a boy that looks 10 may be 20, a lady that looks 80 may be 45.

One of the interpreters explained that within some families (the harder-working ones from the country) a young boy has to work from sunrise to sunset seven days a week all year round with only three major holidays off. If the boy is lucky, like the interpreter, and has been brought up in the city, then he may even get a chance to go to school.

As we stopped to anchor at different spots in the Haiphong Harbor, little sail boats called "Bumboats" or "San Pan boats" continuously followed our ship. Each boat had a family consisting of about five people (average) which performed all their daily tasks right on the boat. Sometimes we would spot boats with chickens and pigs.

Most of the women chew beetle-nut, which is a substance that has a counter-reaction to diarrhea and tends to make their teeth black. And when I say black—I mean black! We have also spotted several men smoking opium pipes which probably makes them very happy. Ha.

Trying to get to the heart of a refugee's illness can be amusing. The doctor asks questions of the first interpreter (who speaks English and French) who asks a second interpreter (who speaks French and Vietnamese) who asks a 3rd interpreter (who speaks Vietnamese and Chinese) who asks a member of the family (the mother) who finally asks the patient (the child). By then, if the patient isn't dead, the answer starts back through the chain of languages.

Two of our corpsmen and one of the doctors have had French in high school and I have been studying a little French on the side, in the effort to help communicate with these people.

The three nurses that came aboard for the trip really proved to be helpful, especially with the two mothers who gave birth. The normal degree of embarrassment and modesty concerning sex differences, which we American boys and girls show towards each other, does not exist with these people. All the babies are breast fed out in the open.

Passing out our gift packages with the rice (and later soap and candy bars) seemed to help establish some friendship with the refugees.

I think I mentioned that we only get one chance every two weeks to mail our letters. As always,

Love, Dick

Hi Mom and Dad,   October 25, 1954
Here I am again with the latest news from the Orient. We are sorry to hear of Aunt Dell's death. It was nice that you could attend the funeral.

On the 17th of October we completed another trip from Haiphong to Saigon with a load of around 3000 Vietnamese. To our credit and satisfaction we had no deaths and only two births during that trip, which is better than

Bringing North Vietnamese refugees out to the USNS *Marine Lynx* on a Navy landing craft

Refugees with as many of their life possessions as they could carry aboard

Two Vietnamese nurses who helped the corpsmen with treatment and language interpretation

A Vietnamese interpreter and officers with their families

average. One of the ships had 5 deaths. We did hit a lot of rough weather which, unfortunately, made about 50 percent of the passengers seasick. It seems like all the potential mothers wait until its about time to unload and then decide to deliver.

Then on Saturday and Sunday we both received liberty in Saigon. Spent most of our time looking around, took a few more pictures, rode all over Cholanh [a city some miles west of Saigon] and Saigon in Rickshaws and went dancing Sunday night. We even went into a cinema and saw an American picture in French dialogue, with both Vietnamese and Chinese subtitles.

We are once again in the Haiphong Harbor. Being that there are five of us MSTS ships hauling refugees, it is difficult for the authorities at Saigon to place the large number of people as fast as we deliver them. So we had one three-day trip only taking the load as far south as Touraine Bay. That trip was more work for us, for we did not have any interpreters or nurses. However, the people in general were much healthier and of the 2637 passengers, we had a lot more adults than children.

We were receiving about one mail call per month, but now deliveries are picking up. The Cleveland Indians faded faster in the World Series play-off than ice cream melts on a hot day. Swept by the [New York] Giants. Isn't that the way of it, though?

Have received letters from Skip Maur and Frank Leonard who says he's looking forward to graduating this coming June.

As always, Love, Dick

Hi Mom and Dad,   November 4, 1954

It seems like all we have been doing for the last week is load and unload refugees. We spent the bulk of the day Monday loading around 1700 evacuees and then, thinking we had received all that we were to get, headed out for Touraine. Well, about half way there we received a dispatch ordering us back to pick up around 800 more Vietnamese soldiers and their families. They had spent the night out on a small LCT [landing craft, tank] loading boat and had been miserable all night packed together like potatoes in a sack. Some of the troops were dark colored, perhaps Indian French. About 30 were French with Vietnamese wives and cute little kids, some looking French and others looking Vietnamese. Being soldiers, they had extra supplies and personal gear that took time loading.

Wednesday morning about seven o'clock we started unloading this same load at Touraine. Here is where things got complicated. The LCT can carry about a 1000 people. So if only one is involved, it takes about three ship-to-shore trips to unload everybody. By noon we had successfully completed the unloading for two LCT trips. With one load remaining on board to yet be sent ashore, we then started loading 3000 more refugees that were to go down the coast to different points south of Touraine. These same 3000 people had been brought down to Touraine from Haiphong only several weeks earlier (some of which our ship had carried). Just why, at the time of their first trip, they were dumped at Touraine rather than carried to their original destination was a puzzle. They were all civilians (mostly babies, children, women, or old men), carrying gear that it must have taken a life-time to gather (big, little, and heavy boxes containing everything imaginable).

Our gangway is only three feet wide and quite steep so you can imagine each of these people, trying to bring their possession on board and at the same time holding onto three or four kids in the process. Naturally, we military guys and the crew members try to help out as much as possible. A lot of the refugee men, who leave bundles down on the LCT, because they cannot carry all the gear in one trip, continually try to go back down the gangway in the effort to get the rest. This, however, we cannot permit because it just jams the gangway and therefore holds up the whole process of loading. It is next to impossible (when you can't speak their language) to tell them that they can go back for the rest as soon as everybody is loaded. Each and every one thinks that surely they have lost vitally precious possessions and will never see them again. Some of them were poultry farmers bringing everything aboard from chickens to ducks. Many try to bring dogs aboard, but the Captain has out-lawed this due to any diseases they might carry. Every once in a while a mother will lose track of one of her children and start to cry. We had a group of Nuns and Priests aboard this trip who, like the people, are all Catholics.

We worked until midnight to get the 3000 loaded and had to wait until morning to finally unload the last 1000. This morning, early, we started unloading part of the refugees (640) at the first port (Nha Trang [South Vietnam]) on our trip south. As far as we know, we were the first ship to carry people to this particular port. Unloading was slow because the French only had LCU [Landy Craft Utility] boats (each of which carry only 150 people). This meant a lot of changing around and securing boats.

Now once again we are headed south and will stop at Phan Thiet [a costal city north of Saigon] and finally Saigon. By Monday we should get liberty for the first time in two weeks.

Today (the 5th) is again our enrollment anniversary which reminds us that only four months remain. Getting pretty short! We hope to see a little of Seattle, possibly more of San Francisco, and maybe even a little more of Japan, before we get out. Who knows?

I am now working in the Record Office for the Medical Section and Jerry is in charge of the Personnel Office for the Military Department [i.e., the small group of naval personnel onboard the civilian-manned ship].

We had a short session of beach parties just before this last trip, of which Halloween was the last day. A pumpkin was erected out of plaster-of-paris and painted real fancy for the occasion. Also had a spooky movie to fit in with the yearly event. Ha.

If Jerry didn't mention it, we have a gift for Dad's birthday, but will hold it until March. Speaking of birthdays, we have had two more babies during this trip and two deaths. One was a burial at sea. I stood in and watched one of the births which I thought was very interesting.

Have you decided yet what to do with the puppies?

Love as always, Dick

Dear Ma and Pa,   November 12, 1954

Since our ship yeoman is being transferred back to the states, and I'm the only guy here with any office experience, they decided to give me his job. It seems like I always end up with anything but what a corpsman should be doing. Anyway I have been busy learning the routine of the ship office. Dick mentioned our difficult back and forth trip around Touraine. They didn't send any nurses or interpreters for that one so we had a ball trying to decide what was wrong with the sick refugees. We had six fathers and 38 sisters [i.e., priests and nuns] on board with enough gear to move a whole monastery. The water has been rough, so the compartments have been a big mess with people vomiting. Although they are doing a better job of cleaning it up, sometimes they just have to wade through it.

Finally received four letters and a big box from you with our dungarees, so there is half our worry concerning the where-abouts of our clothes.

We are bothered by the newspaper articles (world news and the information you are sending) we've seen about our operation out here. Our ships have hauled around 80, 000 refugees (our ship alone about 20,000) out of Communist North Vietnam, but it is the French that are taking credit for it. One of the fellows received a big news clipping from home that described our very operation, but no mention of our MSTS vessels. Our five ships are the biggest transports over here and are, without-a-doubt, doing the biggest bulk of this operation. The only people that seem to know we are over here are our parents.

It was good to hear that Mary Wiles got married. She will make an excellent wife.

Houseboats along one of the many rivers of Saigon, Vietnam

The MSTS [ship USNS] *Brewster* has gone back to the states as well as the *Black* and rumors are that the *Adder* is on its last trip to Saigon and we are about to make our last trip we hope. If so, the *Howse* will be the only remaining ship.

Our last trip was the longest and most drawn out affair so far, lasting about eight days before we got the last people off in Saigon. At our second little stop (below Touraine Bay where 300 were supposed to get off) they came out to get them in a small Vietnamese sailboat. We sat around waiting for something bigger for a whole day for the Master-of-the-Ship refused to unload in such a small boat. When the conditions are rough, its dangerous to try to unload down a gangplank that's rocking all over the place. We ended up taking them on to Saigon.

Dick wasn't feeling well, so he stayed aboard the ship. I walked around, visited some of the French cafes, watched the French dolls stroll around, and ended up in a small dance hall where I tried some jitterbugs, French Waltzes, and German polkas. Ended back at the ship at 11:00 which is our curfew time.

Do you suppose you will have any of the pups left when we get home?

Love, Jerry

A street scene in downtown Saigon

Dear Ma and Pa,   November 24, 1954

Last Tuesday we loaded a gigantic load of almost 6000 and came directly down to the mouth of the river leading into Saigon. Just to be different we unloaded here into small French boats rather than go on in (so that we could pull liberty [go ashore]). Since then we have waited for some kind of action and have been trying to get the ship cleaned up. After the people leave there is usually at least a half inch of solid dirt all over everything. Pieces of straw mats, clothing, paper and food just make it look like one big pig pen. It takes ⅔rds of a day to load, and then to unload, that many people. After we had all the compartments filled, there were still 1400 that had to go out on the open decks. About the second day out we hit some rough water and everybody piled down into the compartments. We could hardly get through to make the sick calls. Naturally everybody got sea sick and the familiar groans of *"Says Sung"* could be heard all over. Another thing that is not uncommon to see is a person vomiting up worms. The other day while making the rounds just before chow I noticed a small girl heaving up one and had to wait for the tail to show. It was at least five inches long and very much alive. After that guess what they had for our chow? Spaghetti, and for some reason I wasn't a bit hungry.

We had five births that last trip making it a total of 15 altogether. Three came within two hours with us having to resterilize all the delivery gear in

A Vietnamese woman preparing a meal

between. Besides the rough water and the huge load, everything went well, because we had four midwives and a number of interpreters.

We are hoping to spend several days in Yokohama, Japan, while having the ship decontaminated. Jerry Ross and another of the corpsmen were transferred to the *Howse* which is supposed to stay out here for another month or so. I will enclose a check as I have been doing.

Love, Jerry

Dear Mom and Dad,   November 30, 1954

Hope you had a good Thanksgiving. After six days of sailing, we have pulled into the port of Yokohama, Japan, on the 30th of November and a decontamination crew came aboard to fumigate the entire ship. Each day it got a little colder. One of the corpsmen lent me a set of blues and Jerry is going to wear his greens.

We finished up our tour of duty in Indo-China with a huge hauling. With that 6000 load all the decks were packed with refugees and their gear along with the ladderways and passageways. There had been some kind of agreement made with the French whereby our aid was to end on the 15th of November. That is probably the biggest reason why our last load was so great. It was the last chance of those Catholic people to escape. Some of the refugees trying to escape by Bumboats from unauthorized Communist areas actually

USNS MARINE LYNX is a C-4 type Navy transport built in 1945 in Vancouver, Wash. She is 523 feet long, 72 feet wide and can cruise at 17 knots. Complete facilities for troop recreation are available on board. Equipped with modern safety and life-saving gear, the ship is part of the fleet of transports and cargo vessels operated by the Military Sea Transportation Service, Department of the Navy.

This Souvenir Post Card One of the Services from Ship's Store Profits

USNS *Marine Lynx*

received Communist fire. Being close enough, they could row to the neutral area where either the smaller LSTs [landing ships, tank] or some other type of vessel picked them up. Whether the French will be able to evacuate all remaining Catholics (an easy 100,000) is doubtful. Anyway, Indo-China is in the past for us. It was interesting—that I can say!

I'm enclosing a check for $67, please take $30 of it toward Xmas gifts for friends and relatives. As we did once before, we will do some shopping in Japan and, if we find an ideal thing for a certain person, we will buy it. I've enclosed the menu of the meal we had for Thanksgiving.

Love, Dick

Reflections

JERRY: I regret to say, as I wrote about my experiences, I often generalized and suggested that all the passengers were the same. In reading some of my comments about the refugees, I feel an apology is in order for some of my remarks. Some descriptions, while accurate, pertain only to the less educated peasants of that time, probably mostly farmers whose economic level and cultural patterns did not equip them for life on an American MSTS ship. The behavior did not characterize the officers and their families. Actually, some of the refugees' actions were very adaptive and creative (as for example their alternate use of the commodes) for people completely removed from their own environment. The stuff responsible for their black teeth, while disgusting to us, may have had a strong medicinal value for them.

After reading the background statement about how propaganda had scared the refugees, it is not surprising that they were shy toward us and our treatment and that we had trouble communicating with them. They were afraid of everyone.

Chapter Nine

Reflections

$\mathcal{A}$s I reviewed our letters and the highlights of the war through the eyes of a number of historians, I was reminded that war is hell and that the Korean conflict was very much a war. The preparation of our story dredged up many essentially forgotten thoughts and feelings. Dick and I felt we needed this final chapter for some commentary and overall reflections. We wanted to express our opinions on a number of aspects of the Korean War.

Unfortunately, Dick passed away on July 21, 1998, after the most ferocious battle of his life—against an aggressive bone cancer. Now, for myself as an ex-corpsman, and on behalf of Dick Chappell, and without pretense of being a historian in any shape or form, I have done my best in this final chapter to reflect on the war in general and to share further impressions.

One can learn the complete story of the Korean conflict by reading the work of such excellent authors and historians as Walter G. Hermes (1966), Gen. Matthew B. Ridgway (1967), Pat Meid and James M. Yingling (1972), Edwin P. Hoyt (1985), Callum MacDonald (1986), Clay Blair (1987), Henry Berry (1988), Donald Knox and Alfred Coppel (1988), James L. Stokesbury (1988), and Rod Paschall (1995). We have read from these authors to refresh our memory of some of the events in the background sections and to ensure the accuracy of our descriptions of them.

Jerry (on the left) and Dick discussing their letters and the war

On Turning Navy Hospitalmen into Marine Corpsmen

One aspect of my participation in the war continues to perplex me. I was never sure how wise it was for the Marine Corps to use hospitalmen as their medical personnel in the thick of battle, rather than Marines trained in the style of army medics.

Although the corpsman's key objective was to tend to the injured, he had to do so in combat action, for which he was minimally trained. Sooner or later, the corpsman was forced to use weapons to defend his own life or the safety of his unit. In the heat of battle, his firepower was counted on, yet in such a case he was like a loose lug-nut on a car's wheel. In my opinion, he was not sufficiently trained to be an integral part of a carefully orchestrated fighting machine—a squad or platoon. As I nearly did in the one incident we have reported here (the treatment of outpost casualties, in the reflections section of chapter 6), I could have seriously fouled things up. Perhaps the present plan—it is still in effect today—works for a career person who wants to be a professional corpsman. But should not fighting marines, rather than "draftees" from the navy, be trained to cover the medical needs of the battlefield?

Rather than shifting hospitalmen into corpsmen, why not give a large percentage of marines a few extra months of training, in battlefield lifesaving? At the risk of sounding facetious, I am suggesting that marines be taught the art of hemorrhage control and of bandaging gaping chest and abdominal wounds, shattered limbs, and ripped-apart faces and heads. Give them special training in pain control, in the counteraction of heat exhaustion and frostbite, in battlefield psychological counseling of the severely wounded and dying, and in evacuating the wounded to safety. Sooner or later, in intense combat, the corpsman is going to be unavailable, and each marine is likely to need at least to help mend his own wounds or those of many fellow squad members.

On the Upside of the Korean War

Before I became a student of the Korean War in 1998, my impression of its validity was negative. The historians stirred my memory of the war and gave me a better picture. I followed the gradual shift in historians' opinions through the 1960s, '70s, '80s, and '90s. Many of the early writers viewed the war as a waste of lives, a failure of American arms, and a conflict that the American people despised and considered forgettable.

The more recent historians speak, in contrast, of the merits of the war from an international point of view. Some suggesting that all the involved nations were more or less winners. Although it was never popular with the American public, the Korean War provided an enormous stimulus to our national economy and raised our prosperity to a new high. It also gave us such an abundance of military power that no postwar settlement thereafter was possible without our involvement.

North Korea, the site of much of the fighting, was practically destroyed as MacArthur pushed northward to the Manchurian border. The UN forces eventually failed to hold all that real estate, and North Korea remained communist. Although South Korea, the other half of the battleground, was devastated, Syngman Rhee's government was saved. The battles in Korea were successful in that they deprived an aggressor (the communists) of unlawful gains and severely punished them for the attempt.

So today, though the war ended in more or less a draw, it is viewed as having been lucrative for most of the "good guys," from an objective, international, and intellectual perspective. The closer we get to the fiftieth anniversary of the armistice, the more historians are saying the war was significant, worthwhile, successful, and just.

Well, all that sounds good, but I have never been very impressed by the idea of war-based prosperity at the national level. I like to see prosperity at the *family* level—for example, when a farm family's crops are fruitful and their dairy herd is highly productive. Ohio farmers do not need Asian wars to be successful.

On the Downside of the Korean War

It has not been pleasant for me to read historians' recent remarks on the negative impact of the war upon the people who fought or lived in Korea and upon the country itself. Obviously, the conflict was a disaster for the Korean people. The employment of war technology by UN forces had devastating consequences. Air and artillery attacks preceding movements of infantry often eliminated whole civilian communities, without regard to who was in those villages.

The United States Armed Forces suffered more than 157,000 casualties in Korea. Nearly 37,000 Americans gave their lives (more than 33,600 were killed in action, and more than 3,200 died from non-hostile causes in Korea and its surrounding waters). South Korea sustained about 1,313,000 military casualties, including 415,000 dead. The casualties among other United Nations allies totaled over 16,500, including approximately 3,100 dead.

China suffered 967,000 casualties, and North Korea 624,000—together, something between 1.25 and 1.5 million killed, wounded, prisoners, or missing. Many UN soldiers accounted for those communist losses by acts of great heroism. But in the final analysis, is any such slaughter really good news? What thoughts, feelings, and dreams have the Americans who participated in those battles experienced over the years about their deeds of heroism?

Perhaps a million South Korean civilians were killed, and several million were made homeless. All told, hundreds of thousands of civilians were killed, wounded, or left dying from disease as a result of bombings, dislocations, flight before the enemy, atrocities, breakdown in the economy, or other war-related disasters. The total number of casualties may well have reached three million or more.

The United States spent about sixty-seven billion dollars on the war, and property worth perhaps a billion dollars was destroyed in South Korea.

Although Dick and I did not have to witness the deaths of any marines for whom we were directly responsible (because we and they were lucky at the time we were on the front line), a few months later the same men were not so lucky. When you can identify even one name, one real man, among the statistics—such as our corpsman friend Coy Brewer, who lost his life over there—it fills you with great sadness. It is difficult to purge your mind of the image of a shattered, lifeless friend. That image taints the memory you prefer to have of that friend: how he grilled hamburgers, cracked jokes, tossed a football, and ran into the ocean at a beach party. That knowledge—that tainted memory—injures your mind and heart forever.

Dick and I did see some of the physical destruction inflicted on the once-beautiful South Korean capital city of Seoul. Parts of it were so thoroughly destroyed that we frankly had no desire to return to it for a second visit.

On the basis of my own negative impressions and the historians' reports, can I personally justify a war that caused so much bloodshed and that destroyed a country to save it? I can only begin to imagine the mental anguish inflicted upon every family that lost a son—every wife and child who lost a husband or father. I can only start to imagine the mental and physical scars that have plagued many of the surviving wounded for more than four decades. I wonder how much the wound that Dick's co-corpsman, Al Fine, suffered has bothered him over the years. No war that kills, maims, captures, tortures, and hides so many soldiers and produces so many homeless people, altogether some three million victims, can be justified.

Yet, the answer to my question is that I have to justify it. This ex–Ohio farm boy and corpsman must believe the war was worth fighting, for if it was not, then Coy Brewer and all the other casualties of that war died or suffered truly in vain.

On the Reasons for Fighting the Korean War

I must focus further on this point. I cannot disregard General Ridgway's personal rationale for being over there bearing arms. Ridgway sent a message (reported on page 649 of Clay Blair's *The Forgotten War*, 1987) to his troops in January 1951, directing that it be "conveyed to every individual assigned or attached to Eighth Army." In it he posed two questions: "Why are we here?" "What are we fighting for?"

The answer to the first question is simple and conclusive. We are here because of the decisions of the properly constituted authorities of our respective governments. As the Commander in Chief, United Nations Command, General of the Army Douglas MacArthur has said: "This command intends to maintain a military position in Korea just as long as the statesmen of the United Nations decide we should do so." The answer is simple because further comment is unnecessary. It is conclusive because the loyalty we give, and expect, precludes any slightest questioning of these orders.

The second question is of much greater significance, and every member of this command is entitled to a full and reasoned answer. Mine follows.

To me the issues are clear. It is not a question of this or that Korean town or village. Real estate is, here, incidental. It is not restricted to the issue of freedom for our South Korean Allies, whose fidelity and valor under the severest stress of battle we recognize; though that freedom is a symbol of the wider issues, and included among them. The real issues are whether the power of Western civilization, as God has permitted it to flower in our own beloved lands, shall defy and defeat Communism; whether the rule of men who shoot their prisoners, enslave their citizens, and deride the dignity of man shall displace the rule of those to whom the individual and his individual rights are sacred; whether we are to survive with God's hand to guide and lead us, or to perish in the dead existence of a Godless world.

If these be true, and to me they are, beyond any possibility of challenge, then this has long ceased to be a fight for freedom for our Korean Allies alone and for their national survival. It has become, and continues to be, a fight for our own freedom, for our own survival, in an honorable, independent national existence.

The sacrifices we have made, and those we shall yet support, are not offered vicariously for others, but in our own direct defense.

In the final analysis, the issue now joined right here in Korea is whether Communism or individual freedom shall prevail; whether the flight of fear-driven people we have witnessed here shall be checked, or shall at some future time, however distant, engulf our own loved ones in all its misery and despair.

These are the things for which we fight. Never have members of any military command had a greater challenge than we, or a finer opportunity to show ourselves and our people at their best—and thus do honor to the profession of arms, and to those brave men who bred us.

Perhaps Ridgway can be grouped with some of the historians who refer to the Korean War as an ideological one. That is, for them it pitted countries with differing ideological positions against each other; nations that aspired to individual freedom and choice were thrown into battle against nations where common men had no individual rights or choice. Men of many nations were dragged into defending an idea of freedom, and paid a high price.

The ideological rationale is powerful. When I arrived on the front lines, I too was sold on the belief that the communists were a menace. Just as Hitler and the Japanese had tried to expand and rule other nations in World War II, the Soviet Union and China had clear-cut aspirations to spread communism worldwide. By invading South Korea they were calling our bluff; there was a strong threat, we believed, that heartless, inhumane leaders wished to overrun our democracies and change our freedom-loving citizenries into nonthinking, obedient masses.

So, with that as our thinking, it seemed best to slam the door on communism in that distant wasteland—which, for all we knew, contained only rice paddies, peasants, and small villages. It made sense to stop the heartless Commies in a remote country thousands of miles away rather than fighting them in the big cities of California, or New York, or Ravenna, Ohio, and its surrounding farmlands.

We like to think that Korea was a war that had to be fought to save free nations from conditions worse than war. It helps to believe it was a just war, fought not because it was convenient but because a failure to resist, a failure to fight, would have been morally wrong. Certainly, all nations owe respect and remembrance to the men who fought so that they could maintain their freedom.

Well, anyway, there we were, assigned to the most noted fighting units in the history of the world. As long as corpsmen had to serve with the marines, I was glad they had a good rotation system for us. We knew that if we could last a couple of months on the front line, we would be moved farther and farther back from the hell of direct fighting. This was not so for the regular fighting soldier, who remained for about ten months in the trenches and bunkers, on the outposts, on "recon" and contact patrols, and in the middle of hill attacks and defenses. Without question, an American marine is like an endangered species. They did not have a chance, like we did, to "luck out" and perhaps be on the line only during a relatively quiet time. Sooner or later each marine's squad, platoon, company, and even battalion would engage in a major offensive or defensive action. Sooner or later, his fighting would shift from small limited-casualty actions to a major, high-casualty one. He could expect, sooner or later, to get wounded or be killed. Many of the marines were professional fighters who expected and lived with those odds; action kept them sharp, and inaction slowed their reactions. I applaud those men. Our nation needs them. But the marines who were draftees, and many infantrymen in other branches of the service who became soldiers because of the draft, feared those odds just like Dick and I did. They were fighting and risking their lives for a war that was poorly explained to them and of uncertain importance to them.

Certainly, my heart goes out to the many unsung heroes of the Korean War—the ones who survived, and the ones who did not. Once again, I trust they were not killed or wounded in vain—that through their courageous effort the door was truly blocked to communism, or at least shut for a while.

I do, however, wonder what reason, if any, the North Korean soldiers and Chinese volunteers were given to fight to their deaths. As many historians have commented, the troops on the north and south side of the MLR slaughtered each other for the control of worthless pieces of Korean real estate. We called them "gooks," "goonies," "Chinks", and "Commies," and I'm sure they had names just as uncomplimentary for us. Does it reduce the nightmares of UN soldiers who killed many of the enemy to think they were heartless, warmongering, commie savages? Undoubtedly, but maybe the communist soldiers fought because they served an uncaring ideology and leaders who misled, brainwashed, or forced them to do so. It does appear that the communist politicians and generals placed little value on the lives of their fighting men. They were readily and pitifully sacrificed. Interestingly, thousands of their men, when released as POWs, did not want to go back to North Korea or China—to their communist homeland.

I wish the Korean War had slammed the door harder on communism, for we had to sail the same ideological boat in the Vietnam War just a few years later, and the Cold War did not end for a decade and a half thereafter. It is interesting that just a short time ago, in mid-1998, President Clinton met with the Chinese leaders and formed an impression of them as nice, friendly people, hardly the gooks of 1950–53. I would like to think the Korean War contributed greatly to that eventual change in the Chinese position.

On the Horror and Hell of War

One has to see the special effects of antiwar, post-Vietnam 1980s and 1990s movies like *The Deer Hunter* (1978), *Full Metal Jacket* (1987), *Platoon* (1986), and *Saving Private Ryan* (1998) to gain some degree of understanding of what it is really like to fight and kill or be killed in battle. Many Americans will not even go to see movies filled with such bloodshed; many veterans probably don't want to be reminded of it.

Perhaps other vets are glad that the public finally does have a way, through realistic movies, to experience a touch of what it is like to fight and suffer the physical and mental wounds of war, or to die and leave a family without a husband or father. It was only after the Vietnam War that realistic movies like *Coming Home* (1978) and *Born on the Fourth of July* (1989) portrayed the impact of war on the wounded.

One of the dictionary definitions for hell is "any extremely disagreeable, unsettling, or punishing treatment, or experience, or the cause or source thereof." War is hell when in fierce combat fellows you have gotten to know drop right and left around you. The fact that you have inflicted tremendous damage on the enemy brings little consolation when your squad or platoon has been essentially wiped out. The Korean War was and is hell for everyone who participated in such events and has lived with memories and thoughts of them since.

My own thoughts relate to how war was hell for corpsmen. I had a traumatic enough experience over there to flood my mind with worry. Nightmares invaded my sleep in my bunker. Often on patrol, stumbling along on a muddy path or sitting in ambush, I would envision mines exploding and severing limbs, destroying facial parts, opening up intestines. I prayed I would be able to cope with all those traumas as a corpsman. On the lookout for attack in a trench or bunker or an outpost, it was hard to not imagine artillery, mortar rounds, and grenades producing horrific casualties; I envisioned with dread massive injuries from hand-to-hand combat or being overrun; I worried about how I would ever get wounded and dying marines back to the MLR. Small things were big things. Rather than being concerned that the ammo for my carbine would run out, I worried I would run out of serum albumin for a badly wounded marine. I feared depleting my supply of morphine, with men all around screaming in pain.

The story on page 41 of the naval doctor and corpsmen in the field who never had everything they needed is absolutely true. Also, it is most unsettling when it is so cold that a marine's blood freezes your hand to his wound. In the battalion aid station chapter I mentioned that I helped treat the wounded legs of a squad member from Easy Company whom I had served with on the front lines. An exploding mine had caused severe damage. We had the doctors and the equipment at BAS to ready him for further evacuation, but it was probably his new corpsman on the line, acting as best he could with limited supplies, in the heat of battle, and the dead of night, who really saved him. The only experience that I think could approach the horror of having your legs

Junior Charity Ball
Portrait Pricing

A. Spectacular Prom $60.00

Guy Alone	Girl Alone	Couple
1 - 8x10	1 - 8x10	1 - 8x10
2 - 5x7	2 - 5x7	2 - 5x7
8 - wallets	8 - wallets	8 - wallets

B. Magical Memories $45.00

| 2 - 8x10 | 4 - 3 1/2x5 | 1 or 2 people |
| 2 - 5x7 | 16 - wallets | |

C. Looking Fine $35.00

2 - 8x10   2 - 5x7   16 wallets   1 or 2 people

D. Just Buddies $20.00

2 - 5x7   8 - wallets   1 or 2 people

E. Friends Forever . . . GROUPS OF 3 OR MORE

Each person in group receives $5.00 PER PERSON
1 5x7   4 - wallets

F. 16 Additional Wallets $10.00

ADD TO ANY PACKAGE EXCEPT E

Markow-Kent Photography
5149 East Cactus Road - Scottsdale, AZ 85254
(602) 264-6404

shattered is having to treat the battered legs and the traumatized mind of a marine who can no longer stand. I remember the despair in that marine's eyes as he struggled to sit up and get a glance at what was left of his legs before we started bandaging them. It was so painful to listen to his questions. What do I tell my folks? Is my girl going to want a guy without legs? I don't remember how I answered him, but I'm sure my answer was inadequate. Having to cope with injuries like opened abdomens or shattered faces with minimal supplies in battlefield conditions, the victims in agony, is without question pure hell.

I knew as well as anyone that human flesh is easily ripped apart by the steel of weapons—that the insult of weaponry had reached a point of overkill—that the human body cannot withstand the blast of machine-gun bullets, the explosion of land mines, the shrapnel of mortar and artillery rounds and grenades, or the scorching of phosphorous and napalm. However, for me, while on the front line, it was easier to cope with the actual casualty than the envisioned one. When the need is real, you act the best you can. The worst fear is the unknown: worrying that you will face a vast number of wounds, all of which are beyond your ability to treat. That was my hell then, and it revisited me in my nightmares for years thereafter.

I thank the Lord that Dick and I never had the ugly experience of firing a bullet, or thrusting a bayonet, through the body of an enemy soldier as was the role of most marines. Surely the experience of watching a life slip away in combat at the hands of their action must have forever scarred the consciences of many marines.

It must have been even more horrible to have partaken in any form of military atrocity. It has to have been soul-wrenching to self-engage, be ordered to engage, or be forced to witness the slaughter of a Korean mother, child, or elderly person—or hundreds thereof—in the invasion of a village, or the killing of helpless, fleeing refugees on and under a bridge, as in the case of No Gun Ri. Such unnecessary killing of the innocent is the greatest horror of war.

On the Vietnamese Catholics

I remember that my first impression of refugees, as we struggled to teach them how to live on a ship, that they were not very bright as a population was gradually but greatly modified. This began as we got to know and converse with several of the interpreters. I came to realize that many factors (differences in culture, lifestyle, and education) accounted for behavior that seemed strange to me.

Some of the interpreters recounted—in fluent English—lives that bespoke very high intelligence and dedication to various professions. I realized that in any group of people there are bright and less bright individuals, highly educated and less educated ones, and people with wide-ranging capabilities and accomplishments.

So in looking back, I hope that every passenger found an opportunity in South Vietnam (during and after Diem's regime) to regroup and lead a successful life. I hope they all survived the terrible Vietnam War that ravaged their country less than a decade later—a war that I am glad was after my time in the service.

On Commemoration of the Forgotten War

As I've said, it was not until the 1980s that military historians and authors started saying, "Hey, wait a minute—maybe the Korean War was worthwhile." I certainly hate the fact that the war of 1950–53 was a forgotten one for many Americans until the 1980s. Even at the time, unless friends or family were involved, few people in the United States cared about how the war was progressing, nor did they for decades thereafter. Since neither side was winning, especially during the last year in the battles of the outposts, Americans got tired of reading about the war. Politicians and generals bickered about strategy; newspapers relegated war news to inside pages. When the war ended, many felt that since the border between North and South Korea remained where it had been three years earlier, little had been accomplished except the killing and wounding of well over a million people. When the decision was made not to fight in Korea to a finish, many viewed the war as a failure.

I regret that I too repressed my thoughts and feelings about the Korean War for years. Our wives have often commented that Dick and I had little to say about our war experiences. Our response was that we preferred to not talk about it. Dick's son, Dale Chappell, has commented that his father wanted to forget the Korean War for forty-four years. I too seemed indifferent, until I started reading our collection of letters and working on our story.

It was not until the early 1990s, fully ten years after the Vietnam Memorial was erected in Washington, D.C., that memorials dedicated to Americans who had fought the Korean War began to appear. Dick's interest in the Korean War was first rekindled when he read about plans for a national Korean War

The National Korean War Memorial in Washington, D.C.

memorial near the Lincoln Memorial. He was pleased when it was con-
structed and dedicated in 1995, and he went to see it soon thereafter. When he
discovered our letters in Mom's basement and began to review them, thus
starting the development of our story, all he wanted to do was remember
it all—loud and clear.

The good news is that many Americans, in many states, have gradually
shown remembrance and respect for the Korean War veterans. The two states
that I know something about are doing so, at different speeds and in different
ways. The memorial picture in Wisconsin is very encouraging.

Wisconsin dedicated some thirty community memorials to Korean War
veterans in the early 1990s. They can be visited not only in large cities like
Green Bay, Milwaukee, LaCrosse, and Sheboygan but also in small towns like
Cuba City, Neillsville, Superior, Tomahawk, Baraboo, Delafield, Plover, and
Eagle. In turn, Wisconsin has dedicated highways to the memory of the Korean and Vietnam War veterans. You are reminded of those wars every time
you travel.

It is my shame that during the long postwar period when only a few
people were fighting to establish those memorials, I too was nearly oblivious.
In Wisconsin I know that it was a very special group of people, many of them
Korean veterans, who accomplished that feat.

The Korean War Memorial at Pacawa Lake in Plover, Wisconsin

The Ohio Korean War Veterans Memorial is located in the city of Dayton, in Riverside Park, overlooking the Great Miami River. Dedicated on September 9, 1995, after a six-year effort, it has engraved on it the names of all the MIAs of the Korean War, from across the United States. The monument also includes the names of all the Ohio vets who gave their lives, the names of all women who served in Korea, and information about the ten major battles. I was glad to hear about this monument for Ohio Korean War veterans.

I am not sure grouping all wars together into one memorial, as is being planned for Columbus, Ohio, is a good plan. Each war deserves a separate memorial. Our local Plover–Stevens Point Korean War Memorial is a great model. As the pictures show, impressive statues commemorate the five branches of the armed forces: the U.S. Army, Marine Corps, Navy, Air Force, and Coast Guard. A family can purchase, inscribe, and dedicate a square for a loved one who served in the Korean War. Some day I would like to dedicate such a square to Dick Chappell on a memorial in his home state of Ohio, in or near Ravenna.

One thing is for certain: all marines who fought in the Korean War deserve impressive memorials. In the Korean War, 4,267 marines and corpsmen were killed, 1,261 died of other causes, and another 23,744 were wounded—twice the casualties of World War I. Only 221 of the 7,190 Americans taken prisoner were marines.

Statues for the U.S. Coast Guard, Marines, Air Force, Army, and Navy at the Plover Memorial

The Korean veterans performed courageously. I hope this story, told in letters, will help awaken readers and remind them of all the young men who fought during that war. Their stories of faithful sacrifice must never die. We must believe that they fought a war of unquestionable value, doing so gallantly in behalf of all the Americans. I certainly commend the unsung heroes of the Korean conflict, be they UN soldiers, North Korean, or Chinese—for I doubt any of them really wanted to confront murderous weapons in bloody, wet, and dirty foxholes, trenches, bunkers, outposts, and rice paddies. I know that Dick and I did not.

On Concluding Our Tour of Duty

We left Yokohama, Japan, on November 4, 1954, after another five wonderful days of liberty in that city, a big army rest and recuperation center. We spent our nights in many nice clubs, dancing with many nice girls. With us aboard, the USNS *Marine Lynx* pulled into Seattle on December 16, 1955, to have its bottom scraped and repainted. We docked at Pier 66 and had Christmas dinner on the ship. We spent the New Year's liberty weekend, and four others, skiing in the Cascade Mountains. We stayed aboard the *Marine Lynx,* working on inventories, as it dry docked for a while in Olympia, Washington.

The following letters brought the news our Ohio parents had been waiting for.

Dear Ma and Pa,   February 12, 1955

Three cheers! Hope this isn't a shock, getting a letter from each of us at the same time. Here is the scoop and it's all good. Yes, we are finally going to get out and almost two weeks early. We are over at the Receiving Station where it takes a week to go through their program of processing. We are scheduled to get our final discharge on the 14th of February—Valentine's Day (and two days before our birthday). We plan on taking in a one-week Colorado skiing vacation on our way home (it's right on our route). We have had such a plan in mind since we took the sport seriously. We will use our travel money to cover expenses. We get out Monday and have a ride set up to go almost the whole way to the lodge (as far as Cheyenne, Wyo.).

They have had us typing discharges (Form 88s) and so we even got to type up our own discharge medical papers.

By the way, we just got the Xmas box and have finally picked up our seabags which we are mailing back home with all our gear.

Love, Dick and Jerry

Hi Mom and Dad,   February 14, 1955

Just call me Mr. R. G. Chappell!!!!! That's *Mr.,* for civilian. Ha. We have received our discharge papers and were paid off by the U.S. Navy. I've received $400 dollars (coming from unused leave, rations and pay, $153 dollars in travel pay, and $100 mustering-out pay) and am sending $250 home in money orders. I'll keep $150 for the skiing vacation. We meet our ride in Seattle and start out for Wyoming tomorrow at 11:00.

Love, Dick

As we hitchhiked across the western states, once again civilians, saving part of our discharge money to pay for a skiing vacation, we dropped in to see one of our service buddies, Bobby Eastman, in Twin Falls, Idaho. He invited us to spend and celebrate our birthday with his family.

After hitchhiking through several blizzards, we were given a ride by a young chap named Robert Pugh, from Denver, Colorado; he also invited us to spend several days at his home. We even talked Robert into driving us the fifty miles up into the Rocky Mountains (Winter Park Ski Area) and ski with us.

We had so much fun during our stay at the Timber House Lodge that we talked the owner into letting us stay three more days after our money ran out. We promised him we would send him the extra money as soon as we got home.

Our final ride was with a drunk, who picked us up so that we would drive eastward for him. While he slept it off, we drove right to our Ohio farm in Ravenna, Ohio. We woke him up, assured ourselves that he was finally sober, bade him goodbye, and greeted our folks. We lived that summer on the farm, working at a small rubber factory in Garrettsville, Ohio.

We found people on our trip home so friendly and trusting that we concluded that the service had not ruined us—perhaps it had bolstered our character a bit.

On the Personal Benefits of Being in the Service

I want to end the service part of our story on a positive note. With the exception of having to participate in the Korean War, the early 1950s was a good time to be an American serviceman. A dollar went a long way. You could have a good weekend of liberty on a ten-dollar bill. You could get by without wheels, hitchhiking a hundred miles on liberty, or a thousand to get home on leave, without fear of being picked up by a serial killer. Servicemen in uniform were welcome wherever they went, be it a football game, a Los Angeles USO dance hall, or a Hollywood roller rink. We saw dozens of great plays, such as *Peter Pan* and *South Pacific*. I loved that part, exploring the East and West Coasts of the USA and visiting much of the Orient (Japan, Korea, Vietnam), all at the expense of the government.

Afterward the government picked up (through the GI Bill) the tab for sending us Ohio twins to college, relieving our hardworking parents of helping pay tuition. Those experiences, along with saving a few lives as corpsmen, made our four-year tours of duty worthwhile experiences. It was a break in the course of our lives, one in which we felt we made a contribution to our fellow men and our country. We met hundreds of Americans in the same boat, of all kinds and shapes, most of whom influenced us in one way or another. Some encouraged us to go to college, find a girl, and get married after we were discharged from the service. I hope we had a positive impact on some of them as well. So, being in the service was one of those things of which I say, "I'm glad I did it, but I wouldn't want to do it again."

On Life after the Service

Since the naval medical assignment I had enjoyed most had been in the physical therapy department of the Bethesda Naval Hospital, I convinced Dick that we should attend nearby Kent State University and study to be physical therapists. However, it was about that time that Jonas Salk created his vaccine, and we thought (wrongly) there might be little need in the future for physical therapists.

Wanting to follow a profession that would allow us to continue caring for people, one to one, we went to see the chairman of the Speech and Hearing Therapy Department, Prof. John Montgomery; Dr. Montgomery was in charge of the academic program and the University Speech and Hearing Clinic. He took one look at us and said something like, "Beat it. There's no way a couple of Ohio farm boys like you can make it in a tough program like this." Well, a stint in the navy and marines had taught us a little about the stuff we were made of, so we ignored his recommendation and entered the program—perhaps hell-bent on proving him wrong. Four years later, we both graduated with B.S. degrees in speech pathology and audiology, cum laude. Kent State's program, one of the finest in the country, prepared us well to serve people with communicative disorders. During the first three years of study, Dick and I lived with Ma and Pa Chappell at the Ravenna homestead and commuted to class and clinic in Kent. By that time, Dad Chappell had milking machines and was managing his herd by himself. We did help during key harvesting seasons with the crops.

Here's an article that appeared on June 6, 1959, in the *Akron Beacon Journal,* under the title, "Life Still Double Take for the Chappell Twins (Both to Be KSU Honor Graduates)":

Another important milestone in the lives of Richard and Gerald Chappell, two of 808 graduating seniors at Kent State University, will be June 13. The pair, identical twin sons and only children of Mr. and Mrs. Walter Chappell of Ravenna, will receive their degrees at the University's 46th annual June commencement.

Richard and Gerald are about equal in academic ability; both will be graduated with special honors. Richard completed his college career with a 3.61 grade average, while Gerald averaged 3.55 out of a possible 4.0.

The Chappell twins, who completed their work in speech pathology and audiology in March, now are speech and hearing therapists. Richard is located in Euclid, Gerald in Lisbon [Ohio]. The only difference between the two right now is that Gerald wears a wedding band. But Dick will even up the score Wednesday.

Gerald is married to the former Christine Cook of Jefferson. She will join her husband in Lisbon next September as a first grade teacher. Richard's fiancé is Janet Cernohorsky of Lyndhurst. Next fall she will teach English and Social Studies in Willoughby Junior High School. Both young women also will receive their college degrees from KSU June 13.

From the time they were born, life has been a series of doubles for Dick and Jerry. They were in the same classrooms through Ravenna Township grade and high school. Their first separation in life came after high school graduation in 1950 when they joined the Navy and were assigned to different units overseas. When their enlistments expired, they again got together and registered at Kent State.

Montgomery, seemingly proud that he could teach the likes of us to be cracker-jack therapists, helped us get excellent jobs—for me, a split assignment in Lisbon and Leetonia, Ohio, and for Dick work in a Cleveland suburb. My two-year teaching experience was virgin territory, in the sense that I was the first speech and hearing therapist for both communities.

Early in my freshman year of study, I met Christine Cook at a university "mixer." By the end of our junior year, we had fallen in love and were married; we lived in Ravenna until graduation.

In my first professional job, I encountered some very severe public-school cases. They were difficult enough to convince me that I had to return to school for more education. I applied for and was accepted to the best graduate program in the States at that time (1962), at Northwestern University in Evanston, Illinois. Prof. Harold Westlake in speech pathology took a chance on me and, along with his excellent colleagues, worked very hard to help me earn a master's degree in preparation for service in a clinical situation of my choosing. While I studied there, for an academic year and two summers, my wife, Chris, taught in the Evanston public schools.

In the meantime, Dick, who had married his college sweetheart a few days before graduation from Kent State University, decided he wanted a master's as well, but in audiology. We thought at the time we might someday set up our own speech and hearing clinic. Dick was accepted at the University of Maryland for one of the best audiology programs in the United States. His teaching staff included three of the top audiologists in the nation. Much of his clinical training was done under their supervision in the Veterans Administration medical complex in the Washington, D.C., area.

Dick's next position as an audiologist, which lasted for about twelve years, was in the Toledo Hearing and Speech Center. By the end of that period, Dick and Jan were raising three children, as were Chris and I.

At the request of Pauline Isaacson, chairman of the Speech and Drama Department at the University of Wisconsin–Stevens Point, and at the recommendation of Professor Westlake, I visited Stevens Point and interviewed as a candidate for a teaching position. Chris and I immediately fell in love with the university, the community, and the state. I was hired to initiate a speech and hearing therapy emphasis. Dr. Gerald Johnson and others soon joined me, and we established an academic program and also a university clinic to serve individuals with communicative disorders.

Those were tough, busy years, but Dick and I and our families always found ways to make many visits to our parents and homestead in Ravenna. For a number of years, our vacations were spent back on the farm taking care of the cows and dogs, while Mom and Pop got away for a few days' vacation of their own.

I took a two-year break from my teaching to earn (by 1968) an advanced degree in the excellent program at the University of Wisconsin–Madison. I was the first graduate to earn a Ph.D. in communicative disorders. I remained in the Communicative Disorders Department at Stevens Point, managing the language-disorders course work and clinic supervision, until my retirement in 1993.

Dick advanced into administration and served for a decade as the executive director of the New Castle Easter Seal Rehabilitation Center. Then he shifted to helping the farmers in his area as a representative of Pennsylvania Farmers Insurance. Dick and Jan bought and lived in a home in New Castle, Pennsylvania. Jan taught remedial reading for twenty years in Mercer, Pennsylvania. Their children—David, Dale, and Cheryl—are all grown now and living their own lives. Cheryl and her husband have two young children. Jan, retired from teaching, still lives in their New Castle home. Dick, following a courageous battle with cancer, died July 21, 1998; he is buried in Maple Grove Cemetery in Ravenna. Dad Chappell is also there, having passed away in his sleep shortly after his retirement from farming in 1979, at the age of sixty-nine.

Mom Chappell continues to live in a home she and Dad built on the Richardson-Chappell homestead a few years before he passed away. She has had some trials and tribulations over the years but remains in good health; she continues to live alone, essentially independent. Our motto for her is,

Ma Chappell in 1996

"Doing great at 88." The farm was gradually sold off and is now covered with commercial buildings.

My wife and I now live out in the country in a wonderful log home in Custer, Wisconsin, a few miles east of Stevens Point. Chris, also retired from years of work in the local library, remains a devoted wife with an unmatchable personality. Our forty acres of woods provide ample space for me to play woodsman and sportsman (hiking, biking, snowshoeing, and skiing) along with our two sons (Steve and Scott) and daughter (Cyndi) and their spouses. Steve and his wife, Kathy, have produced three grandchildren (Anya, and twins Noah and Zachary) to help keep us young and active.

Class Lists and Picture

CLASS 19-51

Honor Student	*Grade Point Average*
Anthony J. Castro	97.503

Honor Roll	*Grade Point Average*
Gerald E. Chappell	97.400
Richard H. Taylor	96.700
Thomas L. Anderson	96.427
Peter H. Susman	95.507

Name	*Home Address*
Robert M. Allman	Lost Creek, West Virginia
Thomas L. Anderson	Wilmington, Delaware
Donald F. Beck	Thomasville, North Carolina
Lopecina S. Bernabe	Minatuan, Surigao, Mindanao, Philippine Islands
William C. Besselman	Canton, Ohio
Coy M. Brewer	Marshville, North Carolina
Harvey Brower	Brooklyn, New York
John D. Carpenter, Jr.	Aiken, South Carolina
Anthony J. Castro	Chicago, Illinois
Gerald E. Chappell	Ravenna, Ohio

Jack R. Chick, Jr.	Austin, Texas
Andrew J. Clyde	Bayview, Long Island, New York
Paul J. Cooper, Jr.	Charlotte, North Carolina
Bobby G. Day	Lacey's Spring, Alabama
Paul P. Denoncourt	Sutton, Massachusetts
Joseph R. DeView	Lapeer, Michigan
Charles A. Duke	Rome, Georgia
Frank E. Duncan, Jr.	Athens, Georgia
Donald C. Ericksen	Brooklyn, New York
Dale B. Flakne	Minneapolis, Minnesota
James A. Ford	Aiken, South Carolina
Charles I. Gehring, Jr.	Fulton, New York
David Greenberg	Baltimore, Maryland
Marion F. Griffin	Moultrie, Georgia
Donald H. Guerrien	Erie, Pennsylvania
Robert R. Heath	Osceola Mills, Pennsylvania
George Karos	Martinsburg, West Virginia
Robert T. Landry	Bronx, New York
Leo J. Lefebvre	Franklin, New Hampshire
David McM. Lightcap	Yazoo City, Mississippi
Mario Masciarelli	Binghampton, New York
William D. McFerrin	Marthaville, Louisiana
John S. O'Connell, Jr.	Chicago, Illinois
Paul A. Pankowski	Brooklyn, New York
Arlen B. Propst	Ranson, West Virginia
Robert Quinn	Newton, New Jersey
Ronald R. Reed	Portland, Maine
Wickman R. Ringley	Abingdon, Virginia
Gerald C. Rollins	Baltimore, Maryland
Donald F. Rowland	Brooklyn, New York
Melvin K. Saunders	Covington, Virginia
Ronald H. Stellwag	Elmont, New York
Peter H. Susman	Hartford, Connecticut
Thomas F. Sweeney, Jr.	Amityville, New York
Richard H. Taylor	Yonkers, New York
James M. Thompson	Elberton, Georgia
Edmond T. Tiernan, Jr.	Rahway, New Jersey
Mark F. Vergot	Steelton, Pennsylvania
Hubert D. H. Wand	West Orange, New Jersey
John J. Wenz	Staten Island No. 2, New York
Hubert J. Yepko	Lorain, Ohio
Peter J. Zabita	Elizabeth, New Jersey
Company Commander	Glenn W. Holtzendorff, HMC, USN

Fleet Marine Training Company 45

Class Adjutant	Thomas L. Anderson, HA, USN
Assistant Class Adjutant	Donald H. Guerrein, HA, USN
CLASS AVERAGE	87.722

Class 20-51

Honor Student	*Grade Point Average*
Arthur C. Kyser	98.016

Honor Roll	*Grade Point Average*
Richard G. Chappell	97.556
Joseph M. Morey, Jr.	96.510
Ronald R. Shatto	96.429
Peter T. Cubberley	96.145
Kenneth W. Eder	96.144

Name	Home Address
Ira S. Ableson	New York, New York
Morton W. Altshuler	Philadelphia, Pennsylvania
Don "K" Autry	Oneida, Tennessee
Albert S. Berdanier	Sabinsville, Pennsylvania
John M. Carney	Columbus, Ohio
Richard G. Chappell	Ravenna, Ohio
Francis P. Choquette	Danielson, Connecticut
Peter T. Cubberley	Chagrin Falls, Ohio
Roger O. Doty	Berwick, Pennsylvania
Francis D. Dwyer	Chateaugay, New York
Kenneth W. Eder	Scranton, Pennsylvania
William Everson, Jr.	Phoenix, Arizona
Charles E. Farrell	Taunton, Massachusetts
George Gassner III	Salem, New Jersey
Gayle W. Herring	Nashville, Tennessee

Edward G. Holson	Washington, D. C.
Martin J. Horgan, Jr.	Rockport, Massachusetts
Robert K. Howell	Staunton, Virginia
William R. Kirkland	Petersburg, Virginia
Marvin J. Kojder	Park Forest, Illinois
Rodney C. Kruse	Hanover, Kansas
Arthur C. Kyser	Birmingham, Alabama
Billy J. Lawrence	Amity, Arkansas
Thomas F. Long	Romney, West Virginia
Joseph C. Lovin, Jr.	Griffin, Georgia
William T. McCormick	Hartford, Connecticut
Glenn H. Miller, Jr.	East Syracuse, New York
Joseph M. Morley, Jr.	Essex, Massachusetts
Ronald P. Moussette	Holyoke, Massachusetts
Robert B. Paysinger	Dellrose, Tennessee
Robert E. Peterson	Omaha, Nebraska
Robert R. Pyle, Jr.	Jacksonville Beach, Florida
Harold H. Schacht, Jr.	Staten Island, New York
Stephen T. Scott	Fremont, Nebraska
Ronald R. Shatto	Mason City, Iowa
Donald D. Slate	Thomasville, North Carolina
Maurice R. St. Laurent	Nashua, New Hampshire
Lenord L. Usery	Greenfield, Tennessee
Lewis A. Van Benchoten	Bellevue, Kentucky
John M. Williams	Mobile, Alabama
Robert S. Wilson	West Hempstead, New York
James L. Witmer	Carlisle, Pennsylvania
Paul E. Wright	West Point, Kentucky
Albert S. Zarrella	Brockton, Massachusetts
Company Commander	Roydon R. McAvoy, HMC, USN
Class Adjutant	Marvin J. Kojder, HA, USN
Assistant Class Adjutant	William Everson, Jr., HA, USN
CLASS AVERAGE	89.816

References

Berry, Henry. *Hey, Mac, Where Ya Been? Living Memories of the U.S. Marines in the Korean War.* New York: St. Martin's Press, 1988.

Blair, Clay. *The Forgotten War.* New York: Times Books, 1987.

Hermes, Walter G. *Truce Tent and Fighting Front: The United States Army in the Korean War.* Washington D.C.: Office of the Chief of Military History, 1966.

Hoyt, Edwin P. *The Bloody Road to Panmunjom.* New York: Stein and Day, 1985.

Knox, Donald, and Alfred Coppel. *The Korean War: Uncertain Victory.* New York: Harcourt Brace Jovanovich, 1988.

MacDonald, Callum A. *Korea: The War before Vietnam.* New York: Free Press, 1986.

Meid, Pat, and James M. Yingling. *U.S. Marine Operations in Korea 1950–1953.* Vol 5: *Operations in West Korea.* Washington, D.C.: Historical Division, Headquarters, U.S. Marine Corp, 1972.

Paschall, Rod. *Witness to War: Korea.* New York: Berkley, 1995.

Ridgway, Matthew B. *The Korean War.* Garden City, N.Y.: Doubleday, 1967.

Stokesbury, James L. *A Short History of the Korean War.* New York: William Morrow, 1988.

Corpsmen

was designed & composed by Will Underwood in 10.3/14 Minion on a Power Macintosh G3 using PageMaker at The Kent State University Press; printed by sheet-fed offset lithography on 60-pound Glatfelter Supple Opaque stock (an acid-free, recycled paper), notch bound in sigantures with paper covers printed in three colors on 12-point CIS stock finished with polyester gloss film lamination by Thomson-Shore, Inc.; and published by The Kent State University Press, Kent, Ohio 44242.